# Social Media Marketing for the Future:

## Strategies for 2020 & Beyond

J. E. Ford

# CONTENTS:

# Overview

There are few things in the 21$^{st}$ Century that have been as revolutionary as the development of social media. Still in many ways in its infancy, the scope and field of social media has changed so much since its birth. As with most powerful forces in society, money is one of the most significant motivators that drives change in the social media realm. The amount of money that is in play and under the control of powerhouses like Facebook and YouTube is staggering. For virtually every business out there, social media plays a role in their industry, audience, and market reach whether they realize it or not. Social Media Marketing is no longer an experimental advertising tool used by very specific types of companies. Social Media Marketing is no longer optional. With over 75% of people active on Social Media, and with the decline in performance of other advertising and marketing methods, Social Media Marketing is often your best chance of reaching your customers.

However, things are not fixed in social media. Things are changing. Just as the platforms and the way people use them are still being established, laws and regulations are also evolving to be more relevant for digital marketing. This fluidity and rapid rate of change makes it difficult to keep abreast of digital marketing trends and patterns. Once you invest your time and resources into building a social media presence based on conventional input, your marketing strategy may already be outdated. An effective social media marketers will understand the importance of adapting and flexing with the pervasive change and not only will they be able to react to changes in the market, but they will be looking ahead and planning their marketing strategy according to the changes that are coming. This will help them stay relevant to their customers and stay ahead of their competitors.

Paradoxically, the best way to beat the competition is to do what they aren't doing. Most companies are way behind the curve when it comes to social media marketing and digital marketing strategies. They are only now getting up to speed with strategies that are already outdated. Large corporations and companies that have been around for a long time are at a distinct disadvantage because they are slower to change. They have a lot of moving pieces and parts that make change more complex. Small companies and startups can be more nimble and have a competitive advantage in many ways when it comes to social media. There are already many resources out there that will help you develop a brand and there are indeed many perennial rules of marketing that apply to social media marketing just as much as they applied to print advertising 20 years ago. However, everyone is playing catch up. All of the marketing resources and books out there are seeking to help you make sense of what's already happened. They're trying to help you take advantage of industry trends that have already matured. You can be sure your competition is already doing the same thing. Your customers are already on to the next thing and before you know it, your methods seem antiquated.

This book seeks to help you develop a future-oriented social media marketing mastery plan. You will learn how to decipher the existing and historical patterns in the industry, how to apply timeless marketing rules to new mediums and technologies, and, most importantly, what the most important future marketing trends are going to be and what they mean for your business.

You will learn about the future of Facebook, Instagram, LinkedIn, Youtube and Snapchat—as well as new platforms you may not be familiar with. You will be able to profile and understand the next generation of consumers that is already at your doorstep. Educating yourself on what is coming will allow your company to flex and adapt where it needs to, to meet the new demand and reach your customers the way they want to be reached. You will be miles ahead of your customers who are still trying to play catch-up with digital marketing trends that are not sustainable. The playing field has never been more level. You have never had more opportunity to get ahead of the curve and take out the competition with intuition, foresight and willingness to plan for the future.

The future is here. Are you ready for it?

# Introduction:

Congratulations on purchasing *Social Media Marketing for the Future* and thank you for doing so. What was once an optional means of reaching out to a small, and frequently young, segment of the market has ballooned into a trillion-dollar industry that is often the key determining factor as to whether a new business lives or dies. Social media marketing has changed dramatically in a short period of time and shows no signs of slowing down.

This level of change makes it difficult to pin down what needs to be done to stay up to date with social media marketing, especially for those who are still getting the hang of the entire process in the first place. Difficult is not impossible, however, which is why the following chapters will discuss everything you need to know in order to get started building a social media marketing plan that you can be relatively confident will last for years to come with minimal alterations. First, you will learn about the predicted future of many of today's social media stalwarts including Facebook, Instagram, LinkedIn, Twitter and YouTube.

From there, you will learn all about Vero, an on the rise social media platform that experts believe may be ready to reach the big leagues. You will then learn about anticipated social media marketing trends in the future as well as those surrounding government regulation, email marketing, and privacy. Finally, you will find tips on cultivating a unique presence as well as a profile of the future of target audiences in the form of Generation Z.

There are plenty of books on this subject on the market, however, very few, if any, are dedicated to discussing trends for the future to help you come up with a strategy that will put you ahead of the curve and keep you well ahead of your competition. That is what this book is all about. Every effort was made to ensure it is full of as much useful information as possible; please enjoy!

# Chapter 1: From the Past to the Future

Over the past decade, social media as a whole has transformed from something isolated to web browsers to a hundred billion dollar industry that more than half the world's population is accessing in some form every single day. With such a dramatic framework already in place, it is only natural to expect the next five years to be full of even more significant growth in the space. Thanks to ongoing advancements in internet infrastructure, the wired and wireless networks (and associated hardware) that make social media possible, the world is only growing more connected than ever before.

The end result will be a sort of changing of the guard in the remaining industries that have not yet felt the impact of social media as well as an even greater social media presence in the average person's life. Despite the fact that the history of social media dictates that something new comes along every few years, many of the platforms discussed in this book have withstood the test of time and, while they are unlikely to reign supreme forever, it is a safe bet they all have a few more years of life in them before they go the way of Friendster and LiveJournal. It also seems evident that some of the trends are here to stay.

While there are new social networks working to rise to prominence all of the time, with more than one discussed in the following chapters, it is important to keep in mind that the current crop of social media all-stars have reach and demographics that their predecessors could only dream of. YouTube, for example, is a direct rival to Netflix, the largest content distribution system on the planet. While something new will ultimately come along, for now, you will see more new startups in the space finding ways to work with these major players as opposed to finding ways to usurp them.

When taken as a whole, the improving dynamics of ever-increasing internet speeds, an app-filled social media landscape and billions of connected always-online devices, it is virtually guaranteed that the next five years will see continued shifts to cultural stalwarts akin to the changes that have come to print, television, and radio over the past decade. As more and more devices that track some form of personal data continue to become more prominent, behavioral shifts are becoming evident with a growing acceptance of the monitoring of personal information, as long as it is at the user's discretion.

While there are always going to be unexpected trends, people and products that dictate where the future of social media takes us, the overarching themes of the democratization of media, portable identity and connectivity will continue to be the primary motivators they always have been. As long as this is the case, it is a safe assumption that the social media landscape of the future will be one that is much expanded, but nevertheless markedly similar, to the social media landscape of today. However, the way in which people conduct business via social media could be dramatically altered. That's what this book seeks to discuss.

## *The ROI of Social Media Marketing:*

For as long as social media has been a household phrase, those in the marketing world have been talking about its ROI (return on investment). Brands have definitely gotten smarter about social media in the past decade, with early adopters driving the conversation and seeing standout profits as a result as the old arguments that social media cannot be used for sales or profit have long since fallen by the wayside. Another facet of this is due to the fact that the social media platforms themselves went and developed business models, varying tiers of advertising and plenty of ways for hungry brands to drive their sales as a result.

Nevertheless, when it comes to ensuring your social media marketing is successful in the long-term, it is essential to look at more than just pure ROI and instead consider the following:

- Driving Sales and Leads
- Driving Research and Development
- Facilitating Customer Service
- Enhancing Public Relations
- Building Community
- Protecting Your Reputation
- Branding and Awareness

These are the areas that can most easily be used to generate viable business goals based on social media marketing. The strategic goal for leveraging a successful social media campaign may be to improve awareness of a given brand or product, or it might be to improve your social media following in general. It could also be used to drive leads through the use of things like webinars and white paper

13

offered up through the most appropriate social media channel.

Regardless of the strategic reasons you choose for utilizing social media marketing, your objectives and goals are always going to have specific outputs, not all of which will be financially motivated. Instead, it makes more sense to measure goals through different criteria such as: the number of negative versus positive search returns when your brand is searched on Google, Q-scores, online sentiment or merely protecting your brand's reputation. While more challenging to measure in some ways, this return can be just as valuable as a purely monetary return.

If you are interested in community building, then measuring the size and scope of the community is a good choice. You could also measure the difference in spending between those who are in the community and everyone else. If you are measuring public relations, on the other hand, then you may want to measure things like the number of key community partners you are engaging with, positive media relation hits and the like to determine the true return of your marketing actions. It is also possible to measure revenue that is generated from new products or features that were generated based on community feedback.

When looking at all of these business drivers, it becomes much easier to see that sales revenue is only one of the outputs that matter and can be broadly connected to several others. Likewise, ROI can certainly be derived from social media, as long as you know what goals to look for. In the end, ROI is just a mathematical equation which means you can count on it to remain the same no matter what. It is simply the difference between the amount of money you spent and the amount of money you made as a result of that expense and marketing activity. If the result is positive then the ROI was worthwhile; otherwise, it is a loss. The end result is most often expressed as a percentage.

When looked at it in this way, measuring social media ROI becomes much more straightforward. All you need to do is look for a holistic approach while at the same time resisting the urge to ignore the soft benefits and metrics that come along with most social media marketing. Most people completely miss the boat here. They get completely caught up in the reporting and added features and benefits that you can often get for free through plug-ins and extensions, and they don't focus enough on the cold hard ROI of their social media marketing expenses and efforts. For those efforts that have the goal of driving revenue, you measure that and calculate an ROI, but know that ROI is not for social marketing overall, but rather for that singular effort. To find success in this field, it is important to focus on the broader return inherent in social media, not just its pure ROI.

## Tips for success

While the possibilities are endless when it comes to the future of marketing via social media, there are a few stalwart principles that will never go out of fashion. Keeping them in mind will help you reap results in the short-term while at the same time successfully planning for the long-term.

Try the 80/20 principle: Also known as the Pareto principle, the 80/20 principle is a simple ratio that explains the idea that 80 percent of your results come from 20 percent of your effort. This is a common refrain among sales teams but is equally true of many languages, including English. 20 percent of the words are repeated 80 percent of the time; it is the same with pop music. This principle can be applied to learning if you first take the time to understand with reasonable surety what the most important 20 percent of a topic is. Again, it is important to only apply this principle when you can be more than 75 percent sure you understand what the most important 20 percent of a topic to be. Remember, a little knowledge is a dangerous thing.

In today's hectic, "instant-gratification" world, multitasking has become the norm. The word multitasking is actually a bit of a misnomer as it actually refers to a process whereby you rapidly shift your attention between multiple tasks. When it comes to learning new information, this is absolutely the worst thing you can do as it is important to focus on the new information as completely as possible in order to increase the odds of retaining the information. Rapidly switching focus is one of the easiest ways to ensure you won't be retaining much information and anything you do retain won't be sticking around for long.

## Use SMART Goals

Regardless of what you are trying to accomplish, setting clear goals for yourself will help to motivate you to actually follow through on them. When it comes to choosing the right goals, ensuring the ones you choose are SMART is always a good choice.

**Specific:** Good goals are specific which means you want to be sure that the goal you choose is extremely clear, especially when you are first starting out, as goals that are less well defined are much easier to avoid doing in favor of activities that provide more positive stimulation in a shorter period of time. Keeping specific goals in mind will instead make it much easier for you to go ahead and power through whatever task you are currently undertaking.

**Measured:** In addition to being specific, you want the goal that you ultimately land on to be one where progress can easily be measured as you go along. Not only will this help you to more easily stay on track throughout the entire process, but it will also make the overall change easier to attain as it will be done in incremental pieces that you can feel good about completing every single time. This incremental process will help allow you to create the types of new neural pathways that you are looking for as they are the first step to creating the types of positive patterns that promote change that you are looking for.

**Attainable:** SMART goals are those that are attainable given a realistic amount of effort. When it comes to social media marketing, your goal shouldn't be to put yourself in a situation where a large group is going to be focused exclusively on you at first, as that is asking too much of yourself. Instead, a better choice would be to set a goal such as making five conversions in a week. In addition to not picking something too difficult, it is important that you don't lean too far in the other direction and pick something that you can do without any real effort. Goals that are too easily attainable won't do anything to improve your social media marketing skills overall.

**Relevant:** It is important that the goal you choose is relevant to your current situation as well as being something that is attainable with only a reasonable amount of effort. Relevance is key to turning the SMART goal system from a one-time thing into a pattern and eventually a life-long habit that you can rely on to help you meet the challenges of life no matter what they may be. Remember, you want these early goals to be as meaningful as possible so that you think back on them regularly and fortify the neural pathways as quickly as possible so they become your brain's default way of acting.

**Timely:** SMART goals are those that have a clear deadline attached. Goals that don't have a clear timeframe for completion are goals that are less likely to ever be completed. Without a clear timetable, you can easily push off what you know you need to do indefinitely. Setting a timeframe will force you to actually confront what it is you want to do and work towards it. The timeframe you choose should be enough to make you hustle, but it doesn't need to be so tight that it is unrealistic.

# Chapter 2: The Future of Facebook

Regardless of how you look at it, Facebook is one of the most successful companies of all time. Despite only being in existence for less than 20 years it is already one of the five biggest companies on the planet with a total estimated worth of about $450 billion and more daily users than any other social media platform. With that being said, it is important to keep in mind that July 2018 marked the first time in three years that the company failed to meet user and revenue predictions. Likewise, the 185 million users in Canada and the United States combined remained flat for the first part of the year, and overall additions were at their lowest point since 2011.

In some ways, this is hardly a surprise as Facebook can only grow so far after a certain point, and the scandals that the company has been involved in haven't been much help. Finally, Facebook front man Mark Zuckerberg had previously expressed his opinion that the changes the company was making to improve its News Feed would naturally reduce overall growth as well.

## *Decidedly profitable*

**Ad space to spare:** Nevertheless, the fact remains that of the three billion people who currently have access to Facebook nearly 75 percent use it on a regular basis which means that devoting time to

Facebook-based advertising is still going to be a worthwhile value proposition. It doesn't matter if you are looking to target an individual group or a wide swath of the market, Facebook has the data to make this type of transaction a reality. In fact, thanks to its mobile app, Facebook is actually the largest overall seller of display advertising in direct competition to Google's previous hold on this position.

**Bots:** Facebook recently began allowing companies to create bots which are automated lines of code that can be used from within the Facebook Messenger app to allow users to do a wide variety of activities such as find out the weather and even buy everything from food to flowers. The bot interface is surprisingly straightforward, and many of the bots react in much the same way a person would, albeit with a list of responses that are programmed by the developer so the conversation rarely gets off topic.

For example, the bot for 1800 Flowers provides you with the opportunity to buy flowers as well as reach out to customer support directly. You can enter all of your relevant delivery details as well as additional options. While more and more companies are releasing their own apps, there is still room in the space for a number of stalwarts which will reap the rewards of a new community when things ultimately settle down. While there is certainly nothing stopping users from performing these functions outside of the app, the fact that it doesn't require interacting with any unique interfaces should be seen as a significant benefit.

Increasing reliance on video: While there is no denying that both watching and sharing video is extremely popular on Facebook, the site is currently working to ensure that this is an even larger part of the overall experience. In fact, it is now possible to stream live video from virtually any device, even a wide variety of drones.

## Improving algorithm:

The fact that Facebook can tell who else is in a picture with you is nothing new, what is new is that soon its software will be capable of recognizing virtually anything that happens inside the picture in question thanks to advanced artificial intelligence algorithms. This will ultimately let users search any of their uploaded pictures using general search terms regardless of whether or not they tagged the photo with the identifier in the first place. This technology is based on the same deep-learning software that powers Google Photos which means this service might be coming to Facebook sooner rather than later.

This technology will ultimately be used to help categorize all of the live video that Facebook anticipates hosting in the near future. This means users will eventually be able to do a search for their favorite sports team, for example, and pull up all of the live video that is currently being streamed that has to do with the team in question.

## Facebook VR:

Facebook is already heavily invested in the virtual reality space as it owns the Oculus Rift, one of the premier virtual reality systems on the market, as well as a portion of the Gear VR which is developed by Samsung for use with Smartphone technology. While the VR market hasn't exactly taken the world by storm since its reintroduction in kerberg has already indicated that he pictures virtual reality be something that people use to socialize with each other like never before. In fact, the Oculus group is already working on a wide variety of ways to help make socializing in a virtual space feel more realistic by using high-tech cameras to study the body language of an individual who is moving through a virtual space.

## Facebook Shop:

While you may not see people using Facebook to purchase items much now, the Facebook shop button is anticipated to see a widespread rollout in early 2019 so it will likely become far more common in the coming months. As the name implies, this addition to the Facebook business page tab will allow users to sell a wide variety of items directly from the page which promises to make directing traffic to your wares a more straightforward experience than ever before.

This makes it even more important to have a good idea of not only what your homepage looks like but your collection page as well. Finding one instance of missing pictures or placeholder text is enough to ruin the brand message you are working so hard to cultivate. What's worse, you run the risk of missing out on potentially viable SEO optimization options.

It is also possible to integrate your Facebook shop with a variety of existing online stores including BigCommerce, WooCommerce, Magento and Shopify.

Ads are still important: While not as much of a sure thing as they once were, traditional Facebook ads are sure to continue to be viable as long as a large portion of the planet's population continues to use the site on a daily basis. This is useful for a variety of reasons, starting with the fact that it allows you to target specific products which, in turn, allow you to determine which types of ads are the most important for your target audience. Additionally, this will ensure that if a customer sees a specific product that they like they will be able to click on it and be taken to that item specifically.

# Chapter 3: The Future of Instagram

2018 was a banner year for Instagram with more marketers turning to the service than ever before. While this influx of interest has brought new lifeblood to the service, it has also seen some new changes which means you will need to be aware of the latest and greatest if you want to continue to see results. The following list of trends is sure to shape the future of Instagram marketing in 2019.

## *Vertical Video:*

If you are still looking for proof that all trends reverse if given enough time, look no further than the reemergence of vertical video. While this was once a clear sign that the person who took the video didn't quite know what they were doing, it is now a burgeoning Instagram trend that is sure only to continue blowing up in the coming year. Vertical video is also becoming more acceptable on other sites including Vimeo and YouTube. All this makes it clear that vertical video is not going away which means now is the time to learn to create and edit them properly in order to ensure that you are ready to capitalize on this trend for as long as possible.

If you haven't yet, then now is the time to learn basic video editing skills, even if you commonly work with a video team as it is always a good idea to understand how to edit down a longer video for an Instagram story. To add extra production value to your Instagram stories consider secondary apps like Storeo or Inshot. There are a few choices when it comes to creating an acceptable vertical video, and you can actually trim down video shot horizontally so it looks as though you were savvy enough to hop on this latest retro trend.

It is important to keep in mind, however, that there is a big difference between natively filming in vertical mode and cropping things later and simply hoping it all works out in the end. The most important aspects of the shot that you need to plan for when it comes to vertical video is that everyone remains clearly recognizable which means not cutting off the heads of anyone in the shot and ensuring that you don't end up cutting out any of the good stuff in the process. Current trends suggest that many people feel as though this type of content is actually more engaging than the alternative which means your marketing efforts will see more views and people will consume longer chunks of the content as a whole.

While shooting proper vertical video is relatively straightforward, editing it can be more difficult than you might expect. If you have already edited video then it is certainly within your wheelhouse, it will just take some practice in order to get things down pat. There are a few ways to go about doing so, starting with editing the content on your phone directly.

If you are using an iPhone, then you won't be able to edit vertical video in iMovie which means you will need to go with a third-party app such as Bolt or InShot which will allow you to create vertical videos that still display in 16:9. If you have some more time or want to do something extra special with your video, then you may want to switch to using iMovie on your laptop or computer instead. This is a must if you are interested in adding various layers to your video or things like graphics or text. Doing so will require you to rotate your video clips after editing and then flip them in QuickTime after they have been exported, but these steps are easy to manage after the first few tries.

Even still, if you are planning on creating a lot of intricate video content, then you are likely better off taking the plunge and going the professional software route with something like Adobe Premiere Pro. While this tier of software requires a fair bit of tutorial before it can be used easily, the end result will be superior every single time.

## Instagram stories with AR Filters:

A major theme of the 2018 F8 Facebook conference was how augmented reality and virtual reality are going to be influencing social media sooner than the public might expect and one such way in which they are future-proofing their services is by offering more and more augmented reality filters as time goes by. Getting in on these options and becoming comfortable with them as soon as possible is sure to pay dividends in the future.

Not only are the face filters that Instagram offers a forward-thinking example of how AR can be used in traditional scenarios, brands, influencers and creators of all types can also create their very own unique variations on these options through the use of Facebook's AR studio. While only a few major brands like Kylie Jenner and Rihanna have used this option so far, you can expect to see more and more similar entities taking advantage of this option in the years to come. What makes these filters so useful from a social media perspective is that they are only available to those who follow the women on Instagram, which means it not only ensures their current fans feel special, it also gives those on the fence a reason to join up that is advertised, for free, every time an existing follower uses the filter.

Many filters often give viewers the opportunity to try out a filter that their friends are using which means that AR Filters on Instagram stories are literally created to go viral right from the very start so expect to see a lot of growth in this area in the next year.

## *Offline events:*

As surprising as it might sound, 2019 may very well see the return of the physical meetup thanks to an emerging trend of Instagram taking key influencers on vacation to specific locations. While this is certainly an expensive option, it is certainly a guaranteed way to generate a large number of likes and to sell a large number of products in the process. Companies like Boohoo, Benefit and Revolve are already seeing results taking a small group of highly curated influencers on vacation to take advantage of their existing followings. What they are doing is essentially forcing the illusion of the "cool" lifestyle by inviting viewers to follow along every step of the way and buy all of the cool things they see. Outside of this new example of influencer marketing, another new trend that is really starting to take off is curated museums of the "perfect" Instagram picture.

The real future, however, lies with brands like Refinery 29 Rooms which blend real-world exhibitions with curated experiences, giving participants plenty of opportunities to interact with the brand in a positive way and also post about it in a way that is sure to get plenty of likes on social media. While creating an offline experience can be a lot of work, it can be an excellent way to gain lots of followers quickly while also generating sales at the same time. It is essentially word of mouth for the modern age. When a customer has a positive experience that is also worthy of an Instagram post then it is far more likely to end up on their page where all of their friends can see and interact with it themselves.

The cocktail bar Her Majesty's Pleasure in Toronto is a perfect example of a business that took this idea to heart. While boasting a reasonable amount of business most of the time, by simply updating their theme and décor to more directly appeal to women between the ages of 25 and 34, they managed to grow their followers by more than 26,000 a serious accomplishment for a small local bar. The beauty of this approach is that you don't need an existing physical location in order to create Instagram experiences, you can simply team up with existing likeminded businesses and ensure that everyone benefits from the added exposure.

## Instagram shopping:

Throughout 2018 Instagram has been releasing and retooling its shopping features, but they are stable enough now that you can expect to see serious traction in this area in 2019 and beyond. Beyond simply tagging products in specific posts, users now have the abilities to tag stories to specific products thanks to the new shopping tab that can be found on the Explore page. Rumor has it that soon brands will be able to link up with influencers directly from within the app and that these influencers will be able to tag specific brands as well as products in their posts.

There are a variety of different ways to make sales from Instagram, each of which will ultimately work better with some segments of the market than others. What works for your target audience may surprise you which is why it is best to try as many different approaches as possible as you never know when you will land on a gold mine. Getting started now will allow you to head into 2019 with a new and improved strategy ready to go.

## *Ads in Instagram Stories:*

As popular as they have become, it was only a matter of time before Story specific ads started popping up and 2019 will be the year that they explode in a big way. Current estimates suggest that around 400 million people watch Instagram Stories each and every day which is ideal because it currently offers a far greater return on investment than a similar Facebook ad due to the reduced costs and comparable reach in some scenarios.

As this is still a young form of advertising, it is important to take as full advantage of it as you can before the price increases to accurately reflect its usefulness. This is the perfect time to try out a variety of different formats for your ads to ensure that your game is on point by the time even more people start paying attention. Rather than cropping an existing photo or creating something entirely new, when it comes to ads for specific stories you can still get away with just adding a top and bottom banner in relevant colors. Taking the time to include mentions, emojis, and texts in the ads will help them look more natural as well.

When considering these types of ads, it is important to keep in mind that when people tune in to Instagram Stories they expect to see casual content as opposed to things that are more highly produced which means you will want your ad to have the same aesthetic in order to ensure that people don't immediately swipe past it. Keywords here should be organic and filter-less videos.

# Chapter 4: The Future of LinkedIn

As with the other legacy social media platforms, the next frontier that LinkedIn is going to explore is going to be video. This is obvious for a number of reasons, starting with the fact that LinkedIn is known to take a majority of its cues from Facebook in the first place. If you need proof of this fact all you need to do is consider how much the latest LinkedIn page resembles the Facebook homepage.

LinkedIn is aware that the future is in video and they are anxious not to be left behind. The site already makes it possible to embed video directly into multiple sections of a profile including both the experience and summary sections for that extra personal touch. Real-time video is next on the list of incoming features along with things like Skype integration to allow you to directly to connect to everyone in your network with seamlessly integrated video.

## *Additional Types of Engagement:*

Another area that LinkedIn has been focusing on in recent months is increasing its baseline level of engagement. It has long been a struggle to get people to check in with the site on the regular when they are not looking for work or looking to update their profile. Instead of having a binary level of engagement, a host of new feature enhancements have gone a long way towards shifting how people see the service and your future endeavors with the platform will need to adjust accordingly. Today's LinkedIn is more than a simple resume; it can be a useful tool when it comes to building a personal brand.

## Improved Integration:

Several years ago, LinkedIn purchased an app known as Refresh that is due to be relaunched sometime in 2019. The purpose of this app is to link your calendar to your social media account so that each of your meetings includes details on everyone you know who is going to be there. This is just one of the ways in which LinkedIn is working to integrate itself into day-to-day activities. Similarly, they are working on a tool that will allow one person to deliver webinars to an audience that can be spread out around the world.

## Decreased Base Access:

In a move to push users towards paying for a premium experience, LinkedIn has been in the habit of removing features from the free version of the site. They will likely continue this trend while also looking to create even more types of accounts with the ultimate goal of getting people besides the standard roster of recruiters, salespeople and the like to start paying for a service they have been using for free for the better part of a decade. The platform's plan for the future can be seen in its implementation of LinkedIn Learning which is a free service to premium members that helps the brain stay in shape and offers high quality education on a wide variety of topics. This all indicates that the future of LinkedIn will almost certainly involve a price tag.

While LinkedIn is likely to continue to change in an effort to remain relevant, it is important to do what you can in order to retain as much of your content as possible. For starters, it is important to back up all of your LinkedIn content somewhere outside of the LinkedIn service. You will also want to get in the habit of doing so every time you make significant changes to your content. You will want to do the same thing with all of your connections as your LinkedIn social network is a valuable asset. Moving these things off-site will ensure that you are always able to get to the data you need without issue.

## *Marketing Strategies for LinkedIn:*

Millions of professionals use LinkedIn in some fashion every single day which makes it a natural choice for a wide variety of marketing opportunities. From building brand awareness to building new connections, generating leads and marketing product LinkedIn can be a valuable tool in your social media marketing strategy.

The biggest difference between LinkedIn and other social media platforms is that it is the only platform where standard marketing practices are forced upon users at all times. In fact, it certainly requires a softer touch overall as the hard sell is considered rude and is generally frowned upon. As this network has a very different audience than the rest, it requires a far more specialized approach if you hope to see results in both the short and the long-term.

**More Finely Targeted Connections:** Marketers are able to specifically target their preferred audience more easily on LinkedIn than with any other social network. Marketers have access to the exact job role, company size or industry that they know typically buys their product which means lead acquisition is essentially a non-issue.

**Remain on the Brain:** Thanks to the way the network operates, marketers who have made contact with a potential lead once can easily remain in general contact until the time comes that the client is interested in making a deal. Likewise, if anything changes on the marketer's end, a simple message on the social media site is a low-stress way to reach out and let the potential lead know that the situation has changed. Potential leads will also be able to easily check in for themselves and see what's what thanks to the ease with which status posts can be created and read.

**Improve Secondary Types of Marketing:** While it may seem surprising, email marketing continues to remain a relevant marketing force as the business world gets ready to move into the third decade of the twenty-first century. Once you are already connected with a potential customer on LinkedIn, it then becomes much easier to write a letter that appears to be personalized that invites them to join your email newsletter. You can only message 50 people at a time, but your success rate will likely be a minimum of 50 percent. Just be sure not to abuse this strategy, one unsolicited request to join a newsletter is likely fine, a dozen, not so much.

When writing this invitation, it is important that you make it as clear as possible just what the reader is going to be getting out of the bargain. While they will be gaining valuable knowledge, unless you are known for giving talks or seminars, what you have to say is likely not enough so don't be afraid to offer a value-add as well.

**Sponsored Updates:** Sponsored updates are likely something that you will want to look into as well. This method will allow you to pay to include a specific post in the newsfeed of a set number of individuals. The biggest difference between LinkedIn and other social media platforms in this instance is that you can target a far more specific segment of the audience including things like groups, schools, skills, job function, job title, company name and more. This will make it much easier to reach your target audience without having to fight against the noise from irrelevant alternatives.

This type of update can also be an outstanding way to promote the type of content that can make you a thought leader in your chosen niche. It is important that any advertising of this type feels extremely well-thought out and includes a call to action as part of the bigger picture. This is because people are tired of traditional adds and will almost always skip past them if they don't feel as though there is anything unique or interesting to see right from the start. Those who are likely to view your content won't sit through something that is purely advertising content. They expect something useful out of the experience as well. By promoting content via a LinkedIn Sponsored Update, a specific firm can target those that will benefit the most from the content in question, generating additional leads as a result.

**Quality content is key:** When creating this type of marketing content, it is important that the end results accomplish two primary goals: The first of these is that it should provide your target audience with something that will make their jobs easier or solve a common problem. Second, it should do something to establish you as an authority in the space. When reached, each of these goals will naturally lead to more business, it might sound simple, but it is the most straightforward path to seeing the results you are looking for.

What's more, meeting your goals will go a long way towards putting you on track to gain the type of momentum that causes LinkedIn to put their own spotlight on your brand. They often feature or curate trending content by highlighting it in one of their categories. This is an easy way to gain a minimum of tens of thousands of new eyes which means it is an effective way to improve visibility that can't be duplicated elsewhere.

Another way to promote this possibility is to join as many relevant groups as possible and do what you can to stay active within them once you join. This will not only make it more likely that a larger number of targeted individuals will see the content that you create, but it will also make it easier for you to get the inside scoop about what your target audience thinks about relevant issues. As an added bonus, you can message anyone who shares a group with you directly, even if you aren't connected which makes it a great way to build relationships with new possible clients.

If you can't find a group that fits your target audience to a tee, then there is no reason not to take things a step further and create your own. Once you do so, you can populate it by going out and joining groups that your target audience is likely to be a member of. Once you have been given member status, you can filter out the undesirables and then send personalized invitations to the rest with a valid reason why the group should exist. Not only does this new group feature nothing but potential prospects for whatever you are marketing, you are the moderator for the group so you can ensure that no other likeminded individuals come along and steal your thunder.

Not only is this new group a great place for you to show your own expertise and generate perceived value, but your approaches also won't feel like spam because they opted into the group. You will also have a natural built-in focus group, email list, core prospects, the list goes on and on.

Ensure the company page is relevant: You should also take the time to ensure that your company page is regularly updated to provide a consistent and concise message for your brand at all times. This means that the content, colors, and imagery need to all be on point and in line with anything that your website and other social media profiles as well. You will want to ensure that this page is regularly updated to ensure that your brand appears busy and making plans for the future. It is important to only utilize a company page if you plan on updating it regularly because having an outdated company page is worse than having none at all. Having an outdated page shows that your brand is out of touch and can't be bothered to interact with people on this particular social media site.

Along similar lines, it is important to use your custom URL for your business page as it indicates your overall level of professionalism and dedication to your clients, particularly those who are in the B2B sector or professional services. This is important because researching and googling new potential acquaintances has become a common practice and having a personalized LinkedIn URL will make it more likely to show up on the first page of search results.

Finally, it is also important to take the time to fill out the most commonly ignored section of a LinkedIn profile: the summary section. This section provides you with a full 2,000 characters to speak to your target audience in a persuasive, direct fashion. You aren't given a large number of opportunities to use the hard sell when it comes to LinkedIn, and this is one of them. It is important to use this opportunity to address the pain points you aim to resolve for your target audience, while also introducing yourself as a person to give your profile that personal touch. This is also a great place to include your contact information, regardless of wherever else it appears on your profile as this information cannot be overstated; the easier it is for others to reach you, the better.

# Chapter 5: The Future of Twitter

Researchers from MIT released a study in early 2018 which looked at the ways in which false information was spread throughout the internet. Their primary takeaway is that misinformation is likely to spread about six times as quickly as true information. From a marketing perspective, this can make it easy to wonder if there is enough fake information already floating around on Twitter to make the possibility of getting any new information out there extremely difficult.

Luckily, it will still remain possible to make a profit from Twitter, as long as you keep the following tips in mind. Before deploying a new strategy, it is important to understand the current state of Twitter to avoid making common mistakes while you still have time to pivot your primary strategy. Twitter is without a doubt one of the most commonly used platforms by advertisers looking to get the word out about their products or services.

Unfortunately, Twitter has been dealing with a number of issues lately that need to be dealt with effectively in order to ensure the process is as effective as possible. Perhaps the biggest issue at the moment is the bots which have taken over in an aggressive way. In fact, about 15 percent of all of the users on Twitter are currently bots. These bots automatically tweet or respond to individuals who use specific words or phrases in their own tweets. While a well-designed bot can be a boon to your brand, using one that is even a little off the mark is going to cause issues these days as so many people are aggressively fed up with them that even the hint of one is enough to make them swear off your brand completely.

As Twitter is hardly the leader when it comes to monthly users, the fact that 15 percent of its registered users are actually bots cuts down on the number of potential people you will reach with any marketing content which is why it is important to adjust your marketing projections accordingly. Bots also make it difficult for a real message to get through as they commonly carry links that claim to go in one direction while in reality sending those who click them someplace far less safe. In fact, studies show that about 60 percent of all the links tweeted out on a given day are done automatically as opposed to by human beings.

While Twitter is making an effort to crack down on bots, many people remain skeptical that this will ultimately end up doing much good in the long run as there is so much false information being regularly spread on the platform. This is because while it may well be possible to stop bots from spreading false news on the platform, stopping real people from doing the same thing is much more difficult.

Thus, the Twitter marketing strategy of the future will need to look for ways to counteract the spread of bots, the middling user growth and the deliberate spreading of false information by real people. While it may be difficult, like any strategy, it can be used successfully if you take the time to focus on ways to play to its strengths while minimizing its weaknesses.

# Be more direct:

With two-way Twitter communication becoming more and more common, it is becoming an increasingly normal thing for a potential customer to tweet at even a mid-sized brand with a question that isn't readily available on their site and expect a response. While it might seem like a waste to answer individual questions in this way the truth is it is actually a great way to invest in the long-term growth of your business.

The fact of the matter is that sometimes individual customers need some extra attention and giving it to them could really help transform them into true supporters of your brand. If you do this regularly enough, then you are likely to develop a reputation as a brand that really cares about its customers which is one of Twitter's greatest strengths. In fact, 85 percent of Twitter users believe that it is important for a brand to provide customer service on Twitter.

Being responsive on Twitter adds a level of transparency to a given brand that helps it seem more approachable and helpful, and this trend is only going to continue into the future. A great example of why this case is Dove, which increased its overall market sentiment score by nearly five percent in just three months by doing nothing more than taking a more active response to potential customers on Twitter.

While the right type of service to provide on Twitter is going to vary by company, there are a variety of strategies you can try in order to generate a better response. For starters, it is important to always request a DM when sensitive information needs to be discussed. Depending on the types of questions that you find your brand being asked, this is one of the few scenarios where a bot can be used without drawing ire. A good example of this is Patron Tequila which offers up a bartender bot that offers up cocktail recommendations based on the provided information. While this might sound silly, it increased the click-through rate of specific tweets to their website by more than 40 percent.

When the truly personal touch is required, however, it is important to start by gathering as much useful information as possible as a means of fully understanding the situation. This may include information the user provides directly or, through the use of a chatbot behind the scenes. You could set up a hashtag for things like orders that will be completed accordingly. Depending on the size of your brand it may even end up making sense to create a secondary Twitter handle that is responsible exclusively for dealing with these types of customer service issues.

Private messages are another increasingly popular means of resolving issues on the platform, and the link for doing so is included directly on every tweet. It is important to ensure your account is set up to accept these types of messages, however, as this is not always the case. This can be confirmed by going to the Settings tab and selecting the options for Safety and Privacy and checking the box to receive direct messages from anyone. With this done you can now add a URL with your own Twitter ID into any tweet to ensure the send private message button appears, letting your users know they can send you private messages. You can create your own private message link by filling in your Twitter ID in the following URL.

## *Create video content:*

As with every other social media platform, if you want to see a greater level of engagement in the future, then you need to take the time to create more video content. While sharing videos on Twitter is hardly a new idea, Twitter is always working on creating new ways that videos can be generated and shared with a Snapchat sharing tool on the way as well. If you don't decide to create video content, then you are likely going to be at a disadvantage because by the end of 2019 video views on Twitter are anticipated to grow more than 200 percent.

The reason for this is the perception that video is more likely to cut through the host of false content generated expressly for the platform. Videos are harder to fake which is why they perform better and reach more people when compared to GIFs, images and links. What's more, video on Twitter is actually more effective than video on Facebook at the moment, with the former outperforming the latter by nearly 40 percent.

One of the ways that Twitter users are going to judge the quality of these videos is by the number of views each has received. While this is hardly a true verification of authenticity, it is enough to provide users with a general idea of how many people think the video is worth the effort to watch as well as how far it has spread which makes it easier to determine if its source is likely legitimate.

In order to rack up as many views as possible, it is important to understand what Twitter counts as a view. In this case, a view is racked up after two seconds of playtime as long as the video is taking up at least half of the available screen. These standards aren't high, clearly, so it is important to make a big splash early with your content and go from there.

For starters, this means you are going to want to keep things short and sweet with about 45 seconds being considered the ideal length. It is also important to ensure you regularly use content pillars which are the core types of content that your brand creates and that your videos fit in with the overall theme you are working to create. Common pillars on Twitter include both inspiration and education.

Videos will begin to play as users scroll over them, the first three or four seconds are going to be the most important overall. What's even better, for those who are using video content regularly, Twitter recently introduced the Video Website Card to make videos that are posted as effective as possible. Essentially, the Video Website Card looks like a normal post until it is clicked on which then causes it to open up in full-screen mode with a copy of the relevant tweet beneath it.

The post then also includes a tag at the bottom of the video along with a header and a link to the website in question. When the user clicks on the video again, it then plays in full-screen and they are provided with a new experience as well. This can include things like having a landing page appear or opening the website directly.

## Forming connections:

While Twitter has always been about forging new connections between users of all shapes and sizes, this becomes more and more difficult as time goes on. This trend is only going to continue as the future unfolds thanks to two main issues: verified accounts and bots. When it comes to bots, the issue is endemic in a system where the value of a given user is represented by the number of followers that person has. Is it any wonder, then, that public figures of all shapes and sizes have stooped to using bots to increase their presumed reach and thus improve their actual reach in the process?

As there is already an entire industry devoted to buying and selling followers it can be difficult to determine a clear course of action moving forward. A good place to start is with TwitterAudit which is a free service that anyone can use to see an overall quality score for a given Twitter handle as well as a verdict as to whether or not the account is real or fake. Another good way to determine the quality of a given account is to look closely at the number and frequency of their tweets.

According to user data logs, the average number of tweets is less than 72 with that number making an account appear as though it may be a bot. If the account hits 144 tweets per day then in most cases the account is being filled by a bot. Twitter bots are created specifically to influence user perception and behavior which is why it is so important that your brand comes off as authentic, engaging, trustworthy and, above all else, human.

The other issue to consider is the kerfuffle surrounding verification. Originally, the goal of the blue checkmark was to show others that a public figure's account had been verified in the interest of letting the public know the account was authentic. While this process is theoretically still in place, it was suspended in 2017, and an improvement or replacement process has yet to be implemented. Verification was meant to be an easy way to verify a voice and identity but it has since become something else, and this needs to change if it is going to have any real validity moving forward.

The program is likely going to be changing to a more open verification process which could help combat misinformation across the platform. If accounts, as opposed to just celebrities and influencers, could be verified it would give users of all types more confidence to interact with all sort of entities, confident that they were not simply communicating with a bot.

## Expansion plans:

Once you have verified that your target accounts are real people, the next step is to find them using Twitter's advanced search functionality. This process can be a little touch and go, but there are a number of things you can do to make it as straightforward as possible.

For starters, you are going to want to pay attention to the difference between the word any and the word all as it is sure to come in handy. Generally speaking, using all will limit the search results while any can be used to bring in more results if your initial search comes up short. When it comes to looking for people, if you know who you are looking for but require a specific tweet to source then you can enter their handle as well as the relevant keyword to improve your odds of success.

You may find some use in searching for places as well,

especially if you are marketing for a local business and want to see what people are saying about the community you are located in. If you are looking to see what people had to say over a specific period of time, then you can use the Dates search which is ideal for seeing the response to an event that already occurred or to the release of a new product. The results to these searches always default to the Top replies, but you can also use the People or Latest option to get the true thoughts and feelings of the masses on the topic in question.

## *Sharing in Real Time:*

Twitter has always been at its most effective when it is breaking news in the moment, and this still remains true regardless of the influx of misinformation it has experienced in the past few years. This is due to the fact that the barrier to entry remains so low that there are still an active group of users continuing to generate content. Likewise, it is extremely easy for a person to retweet something and thus feel as though they are a part of the conversation as well. Due to the character limit, the stories are always easy to understand and straight to the point which is perfect for stories that people only vaguely care about. As users can see how popular a tweet is in real time this issue is only magnified.

One hotly debated trend on Twitter that is sure to continue into the future is how long the ideal tweet should be. To the surprise of many, it appears that longer tweets actually lead to an overall increased level of engagement from followers. The reason for this has to do with simple storytelling as longer tweets typically mean more engaging content. The new thread feature also allows for an even more narrative approach which is why this trend is likely to continue for the foreseeable future.

Threads are especially useful for events that include a series of updates, a multi-step tutorial or long-form interviews; they allow brands to branch out and create types of content that have literally never been seen on Twitter before.

## Where It's Going:

The earliest versions of Twitter were first created in 2006, and the sole purpose was to provide a microblogging platform with a hard cap of 140 characters per entry. The company expanded rapidly at first and filed their IPO in 2013. Since then, Twitter has been evolving in some slow, but hardly subtle, ways. Thes days, Twitter needs to worry about keeping shareholders happy, so it becomes easier than it might otherwise be to predict where the platform is likely going in the next few years.

## New Sub-Apps and Tools:

Twitter may create a news application: Love it or hate it, it is difficult to argue that Twitter hasn't changed the way the average news story breaks in 2018. The app is already part of the conversation when it comes to breaking news which is why it would make sense to break that functionality out into its own app, which can then be marketed accordingly. There is serious money to be made if Twitter can find a way to take ownership of this content in a way the original creators approve of because it could then license this content out, much like the Associated Press does with traditional news stories.

Twitter will likely start offering paid tools: It isn't a secret that reaching a group of employees as quickly as possible is something that certain facets of the market would pay for. As Twitter already has the infrastructure to support such an undertaking it could very well expand into this space with a suite of tools with a strong business focus. It is clear that Twitter needs to either expand or narrow its focus in order to reach beyond its current user base of around 300 million individuals as at this point the only real growth is coming from those who previously did not have regular access to a smartphone and focusing on the business segment is as good of place as any to start.

Twitter will likely start requesting for more user information: In order to continue serving up more personalized content, it is very likely that Twitter will soon start to request more and more information from users in hopes of matching them with content they would be interested in viewing. This would obviously be ideal for advertisers as it will allow them to target even more precise segments of the market, improving their metrics all around.

# Chapter 6: The Future of YouTube

YouTube is, without a doubt, a major force in the content marketing plans of the day and that is unlikely to change anytime soon. There are currently more than 1.3 billion register users on YouTube, and at least 70 percent of those create content in one fashion or another for the site. Current studies estimate that more than 75 percent of all of the traffic on the internet is video and more than half of all web traffic after 9 pm is video traffic from Netflix and YouTube primarily.

With video playing such an important role in social media marketing of all types, the importance of having a strong online video presence is only going to continue increasing as time goes on. From a marketing standpoint, YouTube is especially useful as it provides content creators with the opportunity to form a real connection with the viewer and to really explain the ins and outs of the product or service that is being provided. When done correctly, the average viewer will not only be a converted customer but a profitable pair of eyes on additional videos as well.

First things first, before you can market new content on YouTube successfully it is important to test webpage marketing on YouTube in an effort to give yourself a leg up on the competition as a means of helping your brand reach the upper limits of its popularity.

## *Reconsidering Youtube:*

If you hope to make it big in the YouTube marketing world moving forward, then it is important to reconsider the way you think about YouTube. When it comes to overall importance, it should be considered a second website which means putting as much time and strategy as you would for your primary site.

It is especially important to pay attention to your channel as it is essentially the homepage that ties any and all of your disparate content together in one easy to parse place. Remember, every video that ends up on your YouTube channel strengths the overall effectiveness of your site, and thus your brand, as every video ultimately points back to the channel page and starts the process all over once again.

Since your YouTube page is now being treated as a secondary website, it is important that the rules of good web design apply to this space as well. After all, the more authoritative your channel is, the higher your site is bound to rank. Keep in mind that your videos must remain on topic if you hope to build authority

## *Video Content Refresher:*

As the basics surrounding what makes an acceptable video are sure to change over time, it is important to make an effort to stay on the pulse of YouTube popularity so that your videos always look and feel fresh. Nothing will throw a new user off of your channel for good than seeing a recently posted video look as though it is a blast from the past in an earnest way. For starters, it is important to have clear goals as to what you hope to gain from your YouTube videos.

Viable goals include things like growing the overall viewership of your page or site. Video is a great way to encourage viewers to look more closely at your main site which is the first step to an effective sale or opt-in for your products or services. Using your video to capture leads is another natural choice as it is a quick and easy way to provide a list of benefits that come along with opting in. It is important to track all of your YouTube leads religiously as these are the individuals that are already in the know when it comes to your products or services and a knowledgeable lead every time. When done correctly, YouTube videos are a great way to improve your brand's visibility, and they can even be used to make direct sales via a call to action.

## Sequencing Is Key:

These days viewers are unlikely to give a video 10 seconds before they try something new if it doesn't spark their interest. With so little time to spare it is vital that you sequence your videos correctly right from the start. These days, correct sequencing is all about timing, and the perfect length for a YouTube video nowadays is three minutes in most cases and never longer than 10 minutes no matter what.

The start of your video should include proper branding as well as a proper introduction. The days of low-quality video being acceptable are long past, and the more professional your content appears from the jump, the more likely it is that people will actually watch it. It is also important to introduce yourself and your brand and let the viewers know where they can go to find out more information. It is also recommended to go smoothly from the intro into an explanation of what the viewers will gain by watching the video as quickly as possible. You should state the length of the video, so the viewer is aware if they don't happen to be already.

From there, the bulk of the video should follow through on providing the promised information. Avoid the bait and switch at all costs. Throughout your video, you should do what you can in order to ensure it is as clear and detailed as possible. Finally, as with any good message, you must recap what you have talked about and summarize the key points for the viewer. You will also want to highlight the main areas of your service or product once more and give out the link to your website once again for good measure. It is also important to include a call to action such as encouraging the viewer to make a purchase or to simply subscribe to your channel. Finally, it is important to leave a few extra seconds at the end of your video so that viewers have time to click the link before the next video starts.

## *Improve Engagement:*

Moving forward, YouTube is more likely to be seen as a social networking site as opposed to the simple video site it once was. This means that instead of simply posting content you need to interact with your viewers just as you would on any other social media site. After all, the more likes, viewers, friends and overall engagement you have the higher your videos will rank and the more people who will ultimately see them.

# Tips For Creating Captivating Content:

**Detailed product reviews:** Depending on the goals of your content marketing strategy, reviewing products related to your niche or sub-niche is often one of the best ways to bring in new members of your target audience. A review of a product will naturally slip past the standard defenses that many people put up towards sales pitches while still containing virtually all of the same information of a good pitch without any of the traditional stigma that typically comes along with the process. Remember, a review can help customers avoid wasting their money on a shoddy product while a sales page is considered an especially pushy advertisement.

The easiest way to go about doing product reviews is to focus on a single product or group of products with an exceptionally critical eye. This means you are going to want to single out the various weaknesses of the product or product line as well as focusing on its strengths and what makes it unique. It is important to keep in mind that this type of content needs to come off as unbiased as possible otherwise the illusion will be ruined. This means it is important to intersperse positive reviews with negative ones to allow your target audience to come to the right conclusions about your review integrity. When writing these reviews feel free to include two or three links where the reader can purchase the product if they are so inclined.

**Broad strokes reviews:** Depending on the type of products that are relevant to your target audience, you may find an in-depth review of products to not only be difficult to write but relatively useless as well. Instead, you may want to focus on brief reviews that typically include just a single picture and a few hundred words outlining the product's bullet points before including an overall rating and links to purchase if relevant. These types of reviews are typically most effective with cheaper products where readers just want a little information before making their purchasing decisions.

What's more, these types of reviews are known to generate higher than average click-throughs as users are more likely to click the link at the end in hopes of finding out more detailed information about the product in question. These posts then often include things like round-ups regarding similar products as well as a ranking system of some sort. This is important as potential conversions are far more likely to read one article on 10 items as opposed to 10 articles each focusing on a single item.

**Content that answers questions that exist in your niche:** It doesn't matter what niche you occupy or what products or services that you sell, your target audience is going to have questions. These questions can range from specific inquiries about the products or services you sell, ways to make more effective use of the same or even general questions about the niche that you occupy. In fact, nearly 70 percent of all search engine traffic stems from people asking questions.

With this in mind, creating custom content is almost too easy, all you need to do is keep track of the questions that your target audience is asking, and then answer them. Not only will this help to bring in new users who find your content via a basic search, but it also helps to establish you as an authority in the niche right from the start. This, in turn, will help to build trust in your own personal brand which will then make them much more likely to purchase a product or service from you as it will be seen as a transaction that you can trust.

To get started creating this type of content, the first place to look is inward at the products or services that you sell. If you are always receiving the same types of questions then this is a great place to start, otherwise, make like your users and head to Google to determine a good starting place. Start plugging questions related to your niche into the search bar and see what turns up. Remember, the goal here is to stand out from the crowd which means you can stay away from questions that have already been answered. Every time you come across a question that doesn't have a full page of relevant answers take note, you are one article and a bit of search engine optimization from practically guaranteeing yourself a spot on the front page of search results.

Outdo the competition: If you aren't sure what type of custom content to create, then do something similar to what your competition is doing, only better. While you don't want to be known as a copycat, having a great, similar idea is an excellent way to stay in sync with what the market expects, especially if you are just starting out and have not yet developed a personal style.

This means you are going to want to make a list of all of the sites you view as your biggest competition so that you can regularly search their sites for new content. After you get into this habit, you will then need to keep it up. Not only keeping tabs on the competition, but also the target audience's response to the content, can make it easier for you to understand what works best so you don't waste your time early on doing things that aren't going to prove effective in the long run. Once you have the relevant information in mind, you can then work to reverse engineer a version that proves even more effective than the original. This will also make it easier for you to keep up with what your audience is currently up to including changing goals, interests, priorities, and behavior.

It is important to keep in mind the needs of your primary users at all times. If they feel as though their needs aren't being met then they will search to get them satisfied somewhere else instead. This is why one-upping the competition is so important. It will help to keep your fans consuming your content where they belong. You will also need to keep in mind that while you are doing this sort of thing to the competition, they are also doing the same to you. Never be happy resting on your laurels, always be on the lookout for the next big thing.

# Chapter 7: Keep an Eye on Vero

Of all the various social media platforms looking to take a seat with the big boys, Vero looks to be the one most likely to break into the mainstream. Its focus is on a more "natural" experience that is light on traditional ads. While it has already been around for a few years, the platform has only started to gain traction relatively recently. The exact reason why 2018 has seen such a large jump isn't exactly clear, though both the issues that Facebook and Instagram have been dealing with are likely partially the reason for the success.

If you look at the timeline of search trend popularity for Vero, you will see that it has been steadily growing for the last year, but the biggest spike came as a result of the data breach that Facebook experienced as this naturally lead people to look to alternatives. Its app has already seen more than 3 million downloads, and it was even briefly in the number one spot on the App Store. As a social media platform is only as useful as the number of friends that a new user can add when they sign up, this initial boost of interest may be the shot in the arm the network needed in order to start seeing larger numbers of new users on a regular basis.

## *The Vero Difference:*

While a surface level look at the Vero app will show you something that is superficially similar to Instagram, Twitter, and Facebook except that instead of algorithms determining who sees what, all you get is a chronological feed. Users can post the standard list of links, videos, and photos and also do things like sharing their location and recommend various types of media for other people to comment and like in turn.

Vero is also the type of site with a public manifesto regarding its goals, which makes it clear what the overall goal of the service is as well as who it is for. It believes that people naturally seek connections, but that doesn't mean the user should be the product. The current social media model forces the companies in question to rely on their users' data in order to turn a profit. While currently free to build up a userbase, Vero will ultimately eschew this model by charging a subscription fee which means their users and their customers are one in the same. In theory, this should eventually lead to an improved user experience when compared to the competition which is something the mainstream user can respond to. While common in most markets, the idea that the platform is the product is a revolutionary one for the social media space.

Another unique facet of the platform is the fact that it does not offer any push notifications, and it also surfaces the amount of time that you spend using the app right from the primary dashboard. While this goes to show how committed to the user-first mindset the company is, it also means that those who choose to market on the platform are going to need to be on the top of their game as Vero users will likely do less mindless scrolling than their counterparts for just this reason

## Key Vero Takeaways

It was created due to frustration with the current state of social media: The creators of Vero created this network because they were frustrated with what they considered the pain points of the existing social media infrastructure, starting with the concept of the news feed. Users always preferred the chronological approach to the algorithmic one so that's what they've been given here.

Perhaps the biggest change, however, is the lack of traditional ads. Not only is this sure to be a selling point to many users who are fed up with the advertising creep that has slowly taken over the larger social media options, but it also makes those who use alternative methods of marketing stand out all the more.

There are a wide variety of post options: Posts can be television shows, music, text, video or photos while the app as a whole is geared towards the physical experience which is an ongoing trend that shows even Facebook has too much text for the average user. This ensures that every post you make will automatically populate with at least one picture either from your gallery, automatically scraped from link details online or through your camera directly via the app. Vero also makes it extremely easy to add affiliate links right from any recommendation posts you generate. Clicking on the picture in these cases will automatically take the viewer to the relevant platform to purchase it with a portion of the sale going to Vero as well.

More walls between friends and followers: Vero understands that friends and followers are not the same and gives you the option as to how you want to differentiate between the two. Thus, you will likely only need one Vero account that you can use for both work and business purposes. Vero allows users to classify the people in their social network as either followers, acquaintances, friends or close friends and then gate each post accordingly.

There are also no usernames on Vero so other users will see your first and last name if that is how you choose to create your account. When it comes to your profile picture, you are allowed to use any picture that you like without limitation. When it comes to pictures, in general, you will also be able to automatically add a variety of Instagram-like filters, though these are not required.

Getting around: From the home screen, you will find a variety of icons including notifications, collections, user profiles, chat and search which are all straightforward. To create a new post you will want to hit the "+" button which will take you to the "Create Post" page. This will allow you to choose the type of post you wish to make. You can also create up to three avatars that are then associated with your three primary types of connections, furthering ensuring you won't need to set up multiple accounts in order to truly personalize the experience.

The ground floor: While there are more than 3 million users on Vero at the moment, this is still practically nothing when compared to the 330 million people who use Twitter, the 800 million that use Instagram or the 2.2 billion that use Facebook. Thus, putting a substantial amount of work into the space now, will ensure that your page is a premium destination when people start showing up in droves. This is likely to happen sooner than you might think as new big names are signing up all the time with some of the recent converts including Zack Snyder, Selena Gomez, and Rita Ora. The only place you can currently sign up for Vero is through the Vero app which can be found on both the Android and iOS app store.

# Chapter 8: The Future of Social Media Advertising

While the average user may not feel as though much has changed, the fact of the matter is that social media has changed substantially over the past decade and the coming decade promises to only bring about more of the same. What started out as a way for teenagers to interact online has since gone on to consist of several billion dollar platforms that have the level of reach that marketers of previous generations could only dream of.

If you are planning on making it big with social media marketing in the future, it is essential that you take the time to understand where social media is likely heading next and how current trends in this space are helping to shape the next generation of users. Before looking to the future, however, it is essential to consider the current state of things.

Based on the most recent Pew Research data, nearly 90 percent of those over 18 and under 30 use at least one type of social media. This number drops to less than 80 percent for those between 30 and 49 and then drops to about 65 percent for those under 65 and over 49. Finally, those 65 and older still use at least one type of social media regularly about 40 percent of the time. Currently, about 75 percent of those over 18 use Facebook or Instagram every single day. While this data is promising for marketers, it also paints a somewhat Black Mirror future where more and more people are addicted to the online space. As those in the youngest ranges are using these services the most, it is important to understand them in order to find success in the future.

## Video Is Key:

According to a recent study, in 2019 it is estimated that video content will have a return on investment that is more than 50 percent better than print or images alone. This percentage is likely to only increase from here as video becomes even more prevalent across all types of media and content. It doesn't matter if the videos are leadership interviews, behind-the-scenes content, product testimonials or explainer videos, the important thing is that users are gaining an affinity towards specific brands that will ultimately translate into buying potential one way or the other.

As a marketer, all this content consumption also provides you with all the data you need to understand which channels your audience is naturally drawn towards. This makes it easier to eventually create content that will successfully serve that section of the audience even more readily. The long-term strategy then becomes creating long-form content and then distributing it across the relevant social media platforms.

GoPro is an excellent example of this strategy. They have essentially convinced their users to do their marketing for them thanks to the immediately recognizable style of their user-generated videos. The company then uploads these videos to its YouTube channel, and its more than six million subscribers are then treated to a wide variety of globetrotting adventures. What's more, their clear emphasis on community also works in their favor and gives them the appearance of putting their customers first.

GoPro continues to prove it is a forward-thinking company because doesn't stop at just one type of social media output either. Instead, it also has a very active Instagram presence that is heavily focused on the consumer experience. They encourage the posting of Instagram Stories that are user-generated from users who used the @GoPro tag. This flood of personalized content is what has led GoPro to become one of the biggest brands in the social media space, and it is indicative of what can be done if you take the time to determine where exactly your videos will play most effectively. In doing so, you will be free to capitalize on not only the current trends in   video but also any that come along in the future as well. Regardless of what specific trends you follow, the end result will be a long-term relationship with the community surrounding your target audience that will reap benefits for years, if not decades, to come.

## *Short-Form Storytelling:*

With so many users making regular and repeat use of Instagram and similar sites single-serving content and the storytelling options it provides become more and more attractive and will only continue to grow in popularity in the future. While innately less appealing to marketers than evergreen content, this new bite-sized form of storytelling is already proving to be a big hit with users and the brands and influencers who are early adopters are also seeing success.

As this type of content only lasts a limited period of time, it is only natural that it will take numerous tries before you determine exactly what works for you. Good examples of this type of content that are already on the market include brands like Away Luggage and Everlane which have both done great jobs of capturing user interest through sophisticated, strategic and above all unique, types of ephemeral storytelling.

Everlane hired a group of millennial filmmakers to make a video in a famous ice cave in Canada as an excuse to prove how warm their new jacket was. Not only was the resulting video interesting for viewers to watch, but it also served as proof at how warm the jacket actually was. While this trend is only going to become more prevalent in the coming years, there are likely already examples of brands or influencers doing something similar in your niche which means that inspiration is likely only a few clicks away.

This will make it easier for you to learn what tactics are most effective when it comes to reaching your audience and also the techniques that will help to ensure that your customers are interacting with as many separate parts of the story as possible. This often includes things like talking with customers directly and interacting with them on their chosen social media platform. Direct communication will not only provide you with a variety of useful types of data, but it will also help you to form the types of relationships that lead to individuals becoming brand advocates because they feel that they aren't promoting a brand, but they are also promoting a community.

Of course, it is important to keep in mind in these instances that the types of storytelling that can take place in these scenarios is going to be different from what is possible on other platforms. First and foremost, the content that displayed is far less curated, and the various integrations of the format have the potential to make it more engaging. Stories are already overtaking primary grid activity when it comes to Instagram which means that if you don't learn how to take advantage of this type of content soon, you will, without a doubt, be left behind.

## *Influencers on the Rise:*

Current estimates put the influencer market at a 10 billion dollar per year industry by 2020. Millennials and Generation Z, two big audience groups that will be discussed in a later chapter, are embracing influencers enthusiastically which means if your future marketing plan doesn't include them in some shape or form then you are missing out on a serious potential advertising avenue. Influencers of all types use a wide variety of kinds of storytelling to get their message across which is why their appeal is so universal; there is literally someone for everybody.

This makes an easy way for brands to reach entire communities that they otherwise couldn't all while only working with a single individual or small group of individuals. When it comes to choosing the influencers you are interested in working with it is important to first have an idea of what type of content creation you are interested in focusing on and then go from there. Choosing knowledgeable influencers will make it possible for you to essentially allow them free reign to do whatever it is that they do best. Influencer trends that are on the rise include Instagram Stores that share a unique, immersive experience, a full-spread Instagram grid discussing particular products and longer-form content in the form of beauty, product or fashion hauls.

## Courting Controversy

The recent Nike campaign featuring Colin Kaepernick is only the latest in a line of marketing decisions designed specifically to make waves with consumers. As the issue that Kaepernick so publicly supported is so decidedly controversial, it doesn't matter what side of that particular issue you come down on; it is an undeniably bold move on Nike's part.

Other major instances of major brands courting controversy in recent years include Chick-Fil-A expressing their conservative opinion about gay marriage or the NBA moving a game out of North Carolina to protest a recent state law that made it easier to discriminate against the LBGTQ community. Likewise, Dick's Sporting Goods stopped selling assault rifles, and CVS Pharmacy stopped selling cigarettes, the list goes on and on.

What's interesting about all these examples is how they have bucked the trend that most brands follow of avoiding controversy at all cost. While seeking out the comfortable middle ground makes since when trying to appeal to as wide of a base as possible, going hard on a particular issue in an effort to galvanize support behind the side you favor is increasingly proving to be a viable strategy as well.

First things first, taking a stand shows that your brand stands for something and also stands up for what it believes in. If you are choosing to stand up for an issue you actually have an opinion on then your choice will be easy; otherwise you may want to do some market research first and determine which side is going to generate the greatest potential return in the long run. Choosing a side shows both sides that you are willing to go to bat for your beliefs which generates a net positive amount of good will in the process. There is the potential that it will make everyone consider your brand more trustworthy and loyal.

While this is not to say that you are going to take a stance on every issue that comes your way, it is important to take a stand now and then because otherwise, your brand will gain a reputation as being bland—especially if your niche is naturally adjacent to more than one hot-button issue.

Another useful fact about the marketing strategy of "taking a stand" is that it can be used as a means of reinforcing your authority which is discussed in detail in a later chapter. At the very least it will be a good excuse to show off how much you know about the topic in question and the comings and goings of the newsworthy events that might affect your chosen niche. A good example of this would be staying up to date on recent legal developments that have the potential to change how a relevant industry operates. You would then be able to also create your own content weighing in on the topic and its potential ramifications. As long as the topic is well-researched, it will, at the very least, show that you really know what you are talking about which is something everyone should be able to respect.

Now, unfortunately, there are a few downsides when it comes to taking a stand on a controversial issue as well, the biggest of which is that you are going to lose some business, no matter what. It doesn't matter how minor the issue you chose to take a stand on is, you can guarantee that there are some people out there who are willing to put their money where their mouth is on the issue and abandon your brand regardless of how long they had previously been happy customers.

On the other hand, you will find that a portion of the customers that do stick around are going to feel even more loyal than before. As an example, assume you start with 100 people who are slightly positive on your brand before you choose your issue. Now assuming you don't choose anything extremely divisive then you can expect about 20 of those people to be turned off by your choice, 20 would become even more in favor of your brand and around 60 either wouldn't hear about your choice or wouldn't care if they did. Essentially the process removes those who might fall off your brand at some point anyway while also supercharging a core portion of your audience. Frequently, you will gain new support from people that align with your stance. People who were not loyal to your brand before, may become new faithful customers as a way of throwing their support for a particular stance on an important issue.

After all, controversial topics are controversial specifically because people on both sides believe they are right so passionately that they are unwilling to come to a consensus no matter what. This also means that when anyone researches the topic in question, it is likely that the name of your brand will come up as well, providing you with the potential good press for as long as the issue remains relevant. This means that if you are thinking about implementing this strategy, you will want to choose a topic that is just starting to be talked about to ensure you get as much publicity out of your decision as possible.

Even if the topic you choose to support or oppose doesn't make the mainstream news right away, you will still get some benefit from taking a stand if you post about it on your favorite social media platform as it will virtually guarantee that the space will become a hotbed for discussion on the topic. This will not only serve to make your audience feel more involved, but people on both sides of the issue will feel more invested in the brand as a result.

Choosing the right topic can be tricky, especially if the topic you choose starts off as one thing and then gets co-opted into a cause that you do not believe in. This is why it is important to screen your topics very carefully beforehand to make sure that they aren't going to cross any lines that you don't feel are appropriate. Crossing the wrong line can easily spell death for all but the most resilient brands which is why it is important to be aware of the types of factors that can make it easier to predict these types of issues.

Generally speaking, you are going to want to avoid taking a stand on anything related to a longstanding political debate. For example, making a big show about coming out for or against the death penalty isn't going to move the needle much in either direction except when it comes to the most virulent supporters and defenders on both sides.  Instead, you may find that you get far more traction by tackling a local issue like teacher pay or traffic laws.

Another important guideline is to try and ensure that your business has at least some tangential connection to the topic you are supporting. This doesn't have to be something that is specific to your chosen niche, but it should be something you have a personal stake in. For example, in the previous example having a child in the school district would be enough as otherwise, you may not gain as many diehard followers and you end up losing for expressing the opinion.

## VR and AR

The biggest paradigm shift on track to come about in this space in regard to marketing is the potential inherent shift from a 2D to a 3D interface. Facebook and other companies are already working on creating virtual spaces that respond directly to the spot the user is looking and allowing users to move about in a three-dimensional space.

Facebook is already a pioneer in the virtual space, and it is perhaps unsurprising that content marketing is already being perfected for their space. They are really starting to leverage their strengths especially improved empathy and presence. As an example, rather than a traditional television commercial a car company could make a virtual experience that lasts a few minutes and accurately create something that mimics what it is like to drive one of their high-end vehicles. Likewise, a company that matches purchases with donations like Tom's Shoes could create a short documentary that is far more effective at tugging at the consumer's heartstrings than if the same video had simply been shown on television.

VR is already proving powerful when it comes to eliciting empathy, reinforcing customer loyalty, funneling in new customers and converting those who are only on the fence. In much the way social media platforms changed communication as a whole, VR and AR also have the potential to reinvent the way content, as a whole, is regularly consumed. As these technologies are being created, at least in part, with marketers in mind, you can expect the final product to involve templates that anyone can drop content into, regardless of design or coding skills.

What makes AR and VR so potentially attractive for many people is its potential to alter even mundane errands like grocery shopping where things can be tracked as users move throughout the store so that brands can offer up specific incentives for purchase in real time. Users are already becoming more and more used to constant tracking in the form of digital assistants and the ever-popular FitBit. It isn't much of a stretch to take things one step further and ensure all that data is getting to the marketers who can put it to good use.

In addition, these innovations will open up ways for an entirely new wave of content creators to make money off of existing content by simply converting it to this new format. For example, when visiting a new city, a traveler might pull up an AR tour that includes things like videos, language translation services, and geotagged pictures to name a few, all of which will be prime candidates for their own form of advertising.

Facebook is also working on a type of VR for interoffice communication known as Facebook at Work. The premise of this system is that it will be a closed loop that is unique to the needs of each enterprise client. As most people already have a Facebook account, it is easy to get everyone up and running with the service as soon as the platform is integrated into the existing enterprise API for things like voice calls, conferencing, presentations and more.

If this service really takes off, it will mean the end of work laptops and workstations completely as everything would rely exclusively on eyewear technology to work from wherever they happen to be. All of their data is then synced to the cloud, and any typing that would need to be done would happen with a VR/AR keyboard overlay or from the help of a digital assistant who will accurately transcribe whatever you dictate. The truth is this space is only now being explored which means the possibilities are endless for marketers who get their first.

# Chapter 9: The Future of Government Regulation for Digital Marketing

When it comes to reasons why there should be some type of government regulation over social media, it isn't hard to come up with viable talking points: Facebook's congressional hearings, Russian trolls, terrorism recruitment farms, questionable content targeted expressly at children; the list goes on and on. Changes to the standards that social media is held to are already being suggested in many places around the world which means there is almost certainly going to be some action taken on the topic in the near future.

As social media is very much a venue for self-expression, this leads to a complicated conversation in the United States and elsewhere where free speech is valued above all else. Likewise, while a wide variety of sanctions against Facebook were proposed, very little ended up coming of its hearings which also indicates that the status quo might persist a while longer. All told, for the time being, it seems the old standard is still in effect when people start talking about regulation the things they want to regulate typically involve other people.

## *Negative Effects of Social Media:*

One of the strongest arguments for regulating social media comes in the form of a morality argument claiming that it may be as important as regulating things like of tobacco and alcohol. While this may sound extreme, the argument at play posits the idea that if left unchecked social media will make it much easier for large corporations to control the overall flow of information as long as they can afford to create the right types of content. This will lead to suppression and choking out of those who are supporting positive issues if they do not have the same amount of capital in their war chest to create their own propaganda as well.

While large corporations using the media of the time to crush the opposition in the hearts and minds of the consumer is nothing new, social media also makes it far easier for governments to get in on the action which is only a hair's breadth from a wide variety of oppressive regimes such as what it already appears the governments in Russia and the Philippines are trying to accomplish.

Another lesser-known aspect to consider is how the constant influx of content from social media effects a person's health. The constant stream of notifications and the desire to not miss any new content actually activates many of the same parts of your brain that slot machines use to lure in gamblers, expect in those scenarios someone will eventually win something from the transaction. While this is not inherently damaging to the adult brain, the age at which children start interacting with social media is always decreasing which means this could cause the types of issues that won't be clear for years to come.

The issue is further muddied due the fact that too much regulation can end up oppressing lesser-held but still perfectly valid opinions as it intentionally or unintentionally shuts down conversations that can't happen anywhere else. As there is so much discussion about topics of all types online, it is only natural that a wide variety of diverse opinions would be expressed—expression that might fall by the wayside if too much regulation makes the barrier to entry higher than some people are willing to reach. It is also perfectly possible that the regulation that comes to pass ends up being one-sided and only really helps those in power, further disenfranchising the masses.

It would be difficult to establish who would be qualified to write legislation for social media without limiting future innovation and sacrificing too much of its positive power. Depending on who ends up making and enforcing these rules, the real truth is that they could end up having a wide variety of negative impacts on any side of the issue.

A Curtailed Future:

Another reason to oppose regulation comes from the idea of competition and supply and demand. Too much regulation could also serve to discourage innovation in the space as well. The idea here is that if the current suite of social media services isn't doing the trick, then the best solution may well be to start from scratch with a new batch of services that have learned from the mistakes of the past and created something that solves the old problems from the start. On the other hand, if new entrepreneurs are stifled from the start by nothing but red tape and regulation when it comes to building and growing a new business then why would they even bother.

It is also important to point out that social media under tight control has a working model in the world: For example countries like China who already heavily limit what their people can do and see online. While major online companies out of China like Tencent prove that China can still dominate in this space, it isn't hard to see where the differences in the ethos of the internet come into play.

## *Personal responsibility is key:*

Finally, there are some people that believe that the issue is one that ultimately boils down to personal responsibility. Effective regulation will need to address the idea that people should be accountable when it comes to determining what sources of information they choose to believe. It is not possible to outlaw gullibility, no matter how many problems this might solve. Likewise, the line between providing a space for free speech and one that intentionally makes fraud easier to accomplish is very thin and hard to determine on anything other than a case by case basis.

**Finding common ground:** While the loudest voices on both sides don't seem all that interested in compromise, there are a few logical paths towards reconciliation that indicate a possible middle ground could hypothetically be reached. After all, there is a difference between ensuring social media isn't actively being used for malicious purposes and thinking that the government should have the final say on what can be posted to social media in the first place, the dystopian future that those on one side of the argument seem to fear. Likewise, those same people don't want to allow those with the most funds to dictate the truth by spreading misinformation and shouting over all the opposition. Thus, in any conversation about regulation common sense at least has an avenue to prevail.

# Chapter 10: The Future of Email Marketing

There are a wide variety of trends emerging that point towards the future of email marketing, what follows are those that are likely to be the most important in the years to come.

## *Ads Matter less, Creativity Matters More:*

People Trust ads Less: The days of the average consumer trusting the average advertisement are long past. Decades of being burned by products that turned out to be far less than they were implied to be have created a consumer that is only interested in first-hand accounts from people just like them or content from sources that have done the legwork to be considered truly reputable. This is why more and more money is being diverted into alternative types of marketing, referral partnerships and influencer associations as these are all means that deliver clear value to the consumer. Unless traditional ads start providing this type of value, this trend is only going to become more dominant as time goes on.

More and more attention will be paid to creative approaches: Paradoxically, the most important trend to follow these days may well be aiming to be as unique and creative with your approach as possible. It is important to do your research first and ensure that your approach is likely to resonate with your target audience, but other than that practically anything you can imagine is fair game. It is also important to consider the possibilities inherent in integrated campaigns or by using creative distribution tactics that focus on engaging the audience in little-known or unexpected ways as a means of getting ahead of the competition who is still thinking inside the box.

When it comes to creating unique content that breaks down traditional barriers, it is only natural to break down internal barriers as well. As more and more marketing teams are taking risks and trying new things, those that are forced to deal with the endless red tape endemic in the traditional business world will have no choice but to fall behind.

The fact of the matter is that companies that put up an artificial barrier between departments are only setting themselves up for failure in the long run. The most successful companies are those that are made up of a variety of departments that all flawlessly work together. After all, creating content that is truly engaging doesn't just benefit the marketers, it can lead to lower costs, improved relationships and better talent across the board.

More attention needs to be placed on how the customer communicates: It would be an understatement to say that technology has evolved remarkably in the past decade. By now, the image of a child trying to pinch and zoom a magazine or trying to make a call on an analog watch are commonplace, and most customers tend to act in exactly the same way in that they expect companies to communicate with them. This is why it is so important to understand the communication preferences of your customers so that you don't end up missing out on potential opportunities without even realizing what has occurred.

When it comes to how customers are likely to behave in the future, some analysts believe that about 50 percent of all Google and Bing searches will be made via voice search by 2020. As more and more people come of age in a world run by virtual assistants, it is not hard to picture this type of future coming to pass.

When it comes to automation, these advances are sure to help marketers of all levels scale more easily while also making decisions based a greater breadth of available data which will, in turn, help them save money while at the same time generating superior results. As automation increases, however, it is only natural that the personal connection that used to define many brand relationships begins to decline. As such, it is up to marketers to ensure that they go the extra mile to reintroduce that personal touch. Without a doubt, going the extra mile will always lead to more committed clients that stick around for longer and spend more money as a result.

## Focus on Targeting and Segmenting:

When it comes to utilizing an email marketing campaign successfully, segmenting and targeting the correct portion of the population is a vital part of building the types of guaranteed effective marketing strategies that will see results every time. According to a study done by HubSpot, emails that are properly targeted and segmented are 58 percent more likely to lead to some type of conversion. The profit from the emails that are targeted in this way tends to also be about 20 percent higher as well.

As a whole, email marketing is becoming smarter with an increased focus on those who are prone to actually engaging with content as opposed to those who systematically fail to open any provided correspondence. This, in turn, will free up more resources to target the types of consumers who regularly visit your site and interact with your content. Nurturing these types of consumers will ultimately lead to greater levels of engagement, even if it simply starts with additional emails prompting them to take action.

Interactive and text-only emails: While it might seem surprising, there is an increasing trend towards text-only emails which marks a noted shift from the trend of the previous decades. This is due to the fact that numerous studies show that there are so many variables when it comes to viewing images on Smartphones that it is better to use text-only emails that include links to additional relevant content that contains pictures if needed.

While an email newsletter that is filled with pictures might seem more eye-catching in theory, the fact of the matter is that it comes off to many readers as though they are being bombarded with advertisements which come off as spam. Plain text messages also have a more personal feel as it is very rare that a personal email will contain any embedded pictures. This, in turn, makes them feel less sales-oriented overall while also coming across as more personable and sincere.

Another hot trend in types of emails is increased levels of interactivity. As a means of keeping audiences entertained and promoting engagement, many marketers are working to create emails that encourage new engagement via the likes of GIFs, contests, games, surveys, quizzes, etc. The call to action is then nestled in between the interactive bits giving the viewer more of a reason to stick around and continue engaging in the additional content at the same time.

## Increased Storytelling:

While using either plain text or interactive content approach is a good start, an increased focus on storytelling is also an emerging email marketing trend that is an effective way of grabbing the attention of viewers and ensuring they remain engaged throughout the email. Ideally, the marketing message would start with the introductory portion of the story before tying it into the overall agenda of the email and returning to it now and then while also highlighting the products and services on display, news, value adds and the like that the viewer consumes without thinking twice about it.

When storytelling is combined with segmenting and targeting it allows you to create the type of target story for each portion of your audience that you can be relatively certain will pull them in and maximize your reach. This makes them an almost guaranteed positive return on investment and one that is worth looking into more closely in the future.

## Increased Focus on Mobile:

One of the clearest future trends when it comes to email marketing is an increased focus on mobile-first content. Current statistics already show that more than 50 percent of all emails are already opened first on a mobile device, and this number is only growing. What's more interesting is that of those emails that are first opened on a mobile device is that only about 25 percent are opened again on another device at a later time. The list of stats goes on: Of the over 900 million people who use Gmail as their primary email client, 75 regularly open emails on their phones. What all this means is that the trend is becoming such that, if you don't focus on mobile right out of the gate, you might not get an opportunity to share your message at all.

## Increased Privacy:

It doesn't take a futurist to see that the public sentiment on privacy is only growing stronger as time goes on. In fact, outside of the United States, regulations are already changing when it comes to improved policies regarding the privacy of an individual's personal information. This change in policy will continue to affect the ways in which data is gathered and shared. The European Union's General Data Protection Regulation likely just the first drop in a very deep bucket. While this may not directly affect your email marketing policy, it is important to perform your due diligence and make sure there aren't any holes in your current operating procedure that could leave users' personal data at risk.

While the last decade has proven that predicting technology advancement is a tricky business, some trends are so prevalent that ignoring them is practically impossible. The growing trend towards privacy is a fine example of this. It doesn't take a genius to see that communication options that prioritize privacy are going to continue to gain popularity which means that social media marketing in the future will need to take this fact into account in order to continue to be effective.

## Increased Personalization:

While viewers are becoming more and more trained to give out as little personal information as possible, at the same time they are growing used to consuming an increasing array of personalized content. Luckily, automation is also improving which means that automated emails are becoming more viable as well. These emails will automatically include each user's name, information unique to their account and then details based on the segment of the audience they fall into. Future trends in this space include the ability to sort contacts by "buying  personality" and a wide array of desired behaviors.

The end result is content that has been personalized as thoroughly as possible to ensure that each email feels relevant to their personal thoughts, feelings, and actions. Taking advantage of strategies like these will allow marketers to provide content that feels tailored and personalized without spending all their time crafting bespoke emails.

## Artificial Intelligence:

Some companies are already testing the water in the artificial intelligence space by using it to enhance their email marketing strategies and increase their personalization significantly. In fact, AI is already being used to help with a wide variety of email marketing tasks including things like coming up with killer subject lines, automatically locating relevant pictures and determining how likely a given approach is to lead a segment of the user base to open the email in the first place.

Soon this technology should even be able to offer up the odds that a given email approach is going to cause a specific user to unsubscribe from the list. The demand for AI in email marketing is growing so quickly that it is expected to be a multibillion-dollar industry all by itself by 2025 at the latest.

Adobe has recently released its own version of AI technology that offers up a series of extremely complex algorithms created from dated culled from email campaign responses as well as monitored audience behaviors which found that 60 percent of personal emails and 80 percent of work emails will be opened by the average individuals. What's more interesting, however, is that email marketing was one of the most preferred means by which a brand could contact a potential customer. As time goes on, the algorithms that power AI will only become more powerful and the impact they will have on email marketing all that more profound.

# Chapter 11: Snapchat:

One of the fastest growing social media sites of 2018 is Snapchat, and it is easy to see why as it is one of the most popular social media sites for millennials and Generation Z alike. Snapchat currently reaches about 50 percent of those in the premium 18 – 34 range which means that if you are targeting this group, then focusing on Snapchat marketing needs to become a priority sooner rather than later.

There are a wide variety of ways to advertise on Snapchat, and while some of these options are priced prohibitively for smaller marketers, the range of options means there should be something for everyone. One of the most popular means of advertising on Snapchat that most people see is the Discover tab which provides quick access to trending stories, event coverage, viral topics and the like from major names and major brands. The cost to be featured here is around $50,000, but it is an easy way to ensure you reach virtually all of the daily users of the app.

The next option is Sponsored Lens which appear when a photo is taken in a specific area. When a user holds their finger on the screen, they will be presented with a variety of different sponsored lens that alters their content in some way. While you might not think about these lenses very much, or use them yourself, the fact is they are big business and cost a minimum of $500,000 per day depending on the location. The reason for the cost is that they cover a wide area and generate tons of impressions as they are almost guaranteed to be seen whether or not they're actually used, and the potential for a specific lens to go viral and become extremely popular in the short-term is relatively high.

Snap ads are a more reasonably priced option that places an ad in between longer features on the Discover tab that automatically play while the user is consuming content. These ads last 10 seconds and provide the user with the option to interact with the ad in order to see additional content. This is an increasingly popular trend on the platform, and these ads are already seeing upwards of five times as many clicks as those on other platforms. When done correctly, a Snap Ad blends in with the other snaps the user is viewing which means by the time it is clear to the consumer that it is an ad, it is likely already over or nearly completed. Snap ads currently cost about $1,000 per ad.

Another new trend for Snapchat is Snap to Unlock Codes which are essentially a variation on the traditional QR code that look like a yellow ghost surrounded by dots. When a user snaps this code, they then gain access to unique filters or other special offers. These codes can then be connected to time-limited deals, specific coupons, and similar deals.

If you are marketing for physical locales or events, then a Local GeoFilter is another emerging trend that allows marketers to create filters that are active within a certain location. The cost for this type of advertising varies based on the size of the location in question and the length of time for which it is active. For example, if you were interested in creating a filter to run during the three days of a marketing conference, active only at the relevant conference center, then the cost would be around $20. These can be set up for any location, venues, neighborhoods, communities, and is a relatively inexpensive way to generate brand discussion and exposure.

# Chapter 12: Facebook Messenger Ads

The Facebook messenger app is home to nearly 1.5 billion active users, making it the largest messaging app in the United States and one that is likely to remain viable regardless of how strict privacy concerns become on more traditional social media sites. Currently, around two billion messages are sent through the app each month according to Facebook's own data, and a growing subset of those users are using the app to communicate with businesses directly. In fact, a recent study shows that more than 60 percent of those polled they actually enjoyed getting messages from business and more than 65 percent said they would be fine with receiving more of these types of messages in the future.

Advertising on the Facebook Messenger app comes in several forms, the most straightforward of which runs a sponsored message on the app's home screen. These messages are seen between conversations and are clearly labeled with the word sponsor above the name of the advertiser. If you are unsure how effective this type of advertising might be for your company, there are a number of ways you can test the waters before jumping in with both feet.

For starters, if you have a feeling your customers are likely already using the app, then you would want to include the app in current campaigns using available creative and targeting. Facebook will then automatically do what it can in order to get the best results possible. You will then be able to directly compare results from the

News Feed and results from Messenger in reports side by side.

The next option is to use Click-to-Messenger ads which allow advertisers to run a specialized campaign that asks users to communicate directly via a click-to-Messenger. This makes it possible for consumers to easily ask any questions they might have and even allows the advertiser to provide relative support at the moment as needed. This can be an extremely effective way for brands to show customer's they care and the results speak for themselves as brands with a direct line for question tend to see about 50 percent more conversions on average. The opportunities to communicate directly via the messenger are only going to continue improving as time goes on, making this option an emerging trend to watch moving forward.

Instead of a simple communication option, a call to action button is also an option. A call to action button is similar to a straightforward communication option except that it includes a wider variety of options including things like Shop Now, Sign Up, Subscribe, Watch More, Send Message, Request Time, Learn More, Get Showtimes, Contact Us, Book Now, Apply Now and See Menu. After the conversation is started, the target audience is then provided the predetermined message that you generate at startup.

This then gives businesses the option to interact with each person individually, answering their questions or scheduling appointments via bots or live chat. A great example of this type of service is Sephora who saw a 10 percent increase in successful bookings after implementing a chatbot system.

The next option involves delivering sponsored content directly to active conversations that are taking place within the messenger feed. This is an effective and easy way to provide new details to current users when it comes to things like sales and promotions. Another option allows for the sponsored content to show up within the active conversations feed. This is an effective and, more importantly, simple way of letting existing customers know about relevant sales and promotions. These messages are limited to users who have already connected to your business through the app, however, so groundwork needs to be laid before this option can be effective. Those who will see the most success with this type of advertising are those who already have a fairly large following.

## Chatbots:

There are currently around 200,000 bots active in Facebook Messenger with more coming online every day and it is anticipated that this trend is just now picking up steam. Bots can be used in a variety of ways, starting with being programmed to provide specific answers to a handful of questions. More advanced bots are powered via advanced machine learning algorithms and can respond, in real time, to a variety of evolving conversation models. In addition to the data they are initially programmed with, this type of bot can learn from each interaction it has and improve its responses over time.

Messenger Chatbots are already being designed to increase platform functionality in a variety of ways and to help users complete various tasks without exiting their primary communication app. Deciding to utilize chatbots as part of a marketing strategy has numerous different benefits, starting with the fact that it offers up another layer of personalized experience that doesn't feel forced. Chatbots are ideal when it comes to helping to guiding users to specific products, helping them navigate the ins and outs of your site and creating a user experience that is unique for each customer.

They can be configured to run on your site whenever someone visits, or they can be configured so that specific bots run on various pages to improve conversion rates in very specific ways. Everyone knows that marketing doesn't stop at the customer acquisition phase and chatbots are just the ticket when it comes to keeping people engaged. Chatbots are also excellent when it comes to tracking, and even analyzing, customer purchase data. With access to this data, it is then much easier to ensure your campaigns are targeting the right segment of the audience based on the proper behavior patterns.

If that wasn't enough, chatbots can also be programmed to deal with a majority of the customer service inquiries that most businesses come into contact with on a regular basis. If a website has an FAQ section, then it has enough data to create a chatbot that will often send a majority of users away completely satisfied with the experience. Then, if things get too outside the box, the bot can be configured to either seamlessly transfer them to a live person or take the transcript of the conversation and send the whole thing to the relevant customer support person.

Even if using a chatbot in one or more of these functions takes care of 30 percent of the customer emails that typically come in, this is still a significant amount of time that the customer service and marketing teams have to deal with the types of more complicated issues that still require a human touch.

Due to the fact that social media marketing is so common these days, using chatbots to engage with social media followers is another great way to keep users within the app as much as possible. Jumping between apps is still a hassle in many instances which is why offering bots that do it all within the app is so effective and makes the idea of a seamless experience so appealing to many people.

This, in turn, makes it far easier to streamline the marketing process than it might otherwise be. Bots, at varying stages of the process, can serve to funnel users from the market research stage all the way to the acquisition stage and even beyond. Bots can streamline the process of collecting research and survey data by moving each user through the questionnaire at their own speed which means that overall completion rates will increase and the results will also be more accurate as any confusing questions can be easily answered in the moment. These surveys will still end up feeling warmer and more personal than a more straightforward version as the human touch is not only felt but often enough to swing the results.

While they are becoming more versatile every day, chatbots are not yet ready to completely replace humans in all capacities. For the near future, they will be limited to repetitive, predictable, basic tasks that allow the human members of the team to focus more completely on creative work. Likewise, even the best chatbot is not something that can operate on its own indefinitely, it still requires a handler to check in now and then and ensure everything is working properly and that the bot is still bringing in the latest data. Generally speaking, the success a bot sees will likely rely on the various member of your team working together to generate the sort of thing that solves key problems for the customer as easily as possible.

Likewise, chatbots will not replace a full-fledged human customer service department. Chatbots are great when it comes to solving a single issue, but the current versions still tend to fall apart when things get too complex. In fact, generally speaking, the more singularly focused a bot can be, the more effective it will likely be as well. Much like your landing page, it needs to clearly define one issue that it solves for the client and then figure out various ways of helping it reach its goal. Above all else, a good chatbot is flexible which is why it needs to be easy to tweak to account for userbase changes over time.

Overall this type of marketing provides the opportunity for a level of personalized service that is traditionally off the table for smaller brands. It is not immune to poor use, however, which is why the research phase is so important. Otherwise, you will end up with a chatbot that does little but alienate and frustrate customers.

# Chapter 13: Tips on Cultivating a Unique Presence

Generally speaking, the word expert and the word authority are used interchangeably, this is not the case with affiliate marketing, however, where being an authority provides you with countless benefits and being an expert counts for little, if anything in the long run. Specifically, in this case, an expert is someone who knows a lot about a certain niche while an authority is the person that all of the experts agree is the first stop for information on a given niche. To put it another way, authorities aren't authorities because they say they are, they are authorities because when they make declarations in regard to their niche of choice, other people listen.

While being known as an expert in your chosen niche or sub-niche is impressive, there are plenty of other experts hanging around, but there can only ever be a small number of authorities (by definition). If you can find yourself in this position, then you can expect plenty of eyes on your website and legions of adoring fans. As such, in this position, you will be able to stop worrying about looking for ways to grow your audience and can rest assured that those in your chosen niche will seek you out instead.

A large part of becoming an authority is ensuring that the level of trust between you and your readers is at the point where they can essentially take everything you say as fact. The most surefire way for someone to build their authority is to always be right, not just sometimes, or even most of the time, but every single time you make a definitive statement. When you finally make it to the point where you have earned the trust of those who visit your site, you will want to hold it as the gold standard of importance and never do anything to make these people think less of you.

## *Be Mindful of Tone:*

While you should already know what type of content your target audience will be expecting, the way in which you present this information is going to be equally vital when it comes to showing them that you are just alike, except for the fact that you know more than they do. To accomplish this task, you are going to want to make an extra effort to get into their minds, speak as they speak, think like they think and use the same references that they use to relate to one another. The easiest way to do so is to consult your demographic data and pick the largest section of it to adopt as your own.

If your target audience is under 30, then the best way to ensure that you are all on the same page is to visit YouTube.com and listen to the current tastemakers on the niche in question. If you have a niche that is focused more on those over 30, then the time you spent studying the niche should be enough to push you in the right direction. Assuming your target audience is younger, then you will want to watch videos made by content creators with the most views as this shows that they are doing something that the target audience really responds to. Understanding the sound of your target audience will make your claim to authority more believable because you will sound like a peer rather than a researcher.

Once you have the language and tone down pat, the next thing you will need to do is to go over the image you are presenting to your target audience with a fine-tooth comb. Additionally, you will want to consider what, aside from being an authority, you are trying to convince your target audience of and what you are trying to get them to do.

Tones to try
•        Informal: It is best not to start out with an informal tone right out of the gate as new readers can be put off by what can feel like an unearned familiarity. It is fine to adopt it over time; however, you will need to be careful to ensure you maintain your authority at the same time. The best way to do so is to ensure you remain passionate and enthusiastic about your topic while mixing in more detailed insight with the more relaxed phrasing.

•        Promotional: While you will certainly want to promote new products or services as they come online, it is easy to go back to this well far too often if you are not careful which means it is important to be especially cautious about rolling out this type of content early on as you don't want those who stumble across your site to assume it is full of nothing but longer advertisements for your products. Regardless of the content you are creating, it is important to ensure you always maintain your authority throughout by including specific, niche reasons, that make the products or services that you are selling worth your customers' time.

•        Formal: This is the tone you are likely going to want to start with when you start creating content for your business blog. While it is certainly appropriate during the early days, you are likely going to want to slip into something at least a little more informal over time because you want your customers to feel as though they are talking to a friend when they interact with your content, not as though they are being lectured at. While this is an easy way to make it sound as though you are an authority figure, it is the type of authority figure that people listen to because they are forced too, not because they want to.

Consider your voice: Every content creator has a unique voice, a "one -of-a-kind" perspective on the world that comes through in their word choice and their phrasing. In an extremely competitive online environment properly honing your tone can be the difference between being an authority and being just another faceless expert. You are what sets your content apart from any other, do everything you can to ensure it is unique and compelling as possible. If you aren't sure what the right voice for you is, consider the following.

The best place to start is by making a list of all the words that you feel other people would use to describe you. You should spend some time on each of these words and consider how you might make each as clear as possible when it comes to showcasing your personality in what you write. From there, you may be able to add in the written equivalent of any unique speech patterns that you have. These can be difficult to pick out for yourself, which means you are likely going to need some outside input for the best results. You can express these types of things including the sentence structure that you use, the way you separate your paragraphs, the length of your sentences and more. It is perfectly alright if you can't come up with much right now, the longer you keep at it, the more unique your writing will naturally become.

If you can't come up with much of a voice early on, it is important to let it develop naturally rather than forcing it. Having a forced voice will only limit your voice from developing naturally, and essentially paint you into a corner as if you change it once people have gotten used to it you will risk losing their trust.

## Share What You Are Reading:

Another great way to build up the idea that you are an authority in your field is to share what you have been reading. You are taking all of this time learning about the ins and outs of your portion of your niche, you may as well brag a little as it will only make readers think more of you. Dropping a list of names they have never heard of will help cement the idea that you really know what you are talking about.

Before you share the sources of the information you are iterating upon, it is important to vet them thoroughly to ensure everything is as valid as it first appears. Especially early on, you don't want to accidentally stumble upon a so-called expert that is really a fraud that the community as a whole dismissed years ago. Specifically, this means understanding just who created any and all content you plan on referencing, along with their general level of authority within the niche as a whole.

If you pick a source that is reliable, then you can guarantee that it will be easy to verify, while also helping you to ensure you aren't accidentally opening a well-known can of worms within the niche community. While this will certainly take some work, if doing so ends up saving your burgeoning career as an authority within your niche then it will be well worth it.

## Spread the Word:

After you have dutifully created content for several months, you will finally have all the pieces in place to show your niche audience the extent of your authority. To get started, you are going to want to become a regular presence on the most popular forums where people gather to discuss the niche. This means you are going to want to join the forums and regularly join the conversation, answer questions and create posts that other people approve of. Making sure to credit your site with the information each time you do.

During this stage it is important to not pander for any of your products and services at this time, becoming an authority isn't about direct marketing like that, the additional sales are something that happens organically and trying to force it will only delay or stagnate the process. After you start seeing forward momentum and increased traffic from all your hard work, you are going to want to implement the final stage of the plan, which means you are going to want to make sure everything about your site and its content is in tip-top shape before you do.

Once you are ready to really put your best foot forward, the final thing you will want to do is to seek out the websites of other experts in the niche and strike up a conversation. Once you have made nice with the neighbors, the next thing you will do is offer to do them a favor; specifically, you will offer to write them a guest blog. As you will no doubt know by this point, keeping a blog can be a significant strain if you don't stick to a strict plan, which means the other experts will likely gladly take you up on your offer.

This will not only make their lives easier in terms of content creation, but it will also establish you as an authority in the niche to that expert's audience because of your broad reach. Once you have reached out to a new audience, it is important to continue interacting with them in a way that will make them want to subscribe to your own newsletter as opposed to getting their information secondhand. This means creating an active social media presence and maintaining it in the long term. Just like a blog, having an active social media presence that reflects your authoritative status is important to looking professional and having a stale social media pages indicates that you are no longer on the top of your game.

While you can repost content as part of your social media presence, you need to really take advantage of the social aspect of the platform and make as many direct connections as you can make. It is one thing to be the type of authority that puts out decrees from an ivory tower; it is much more effective to be an authority that is seen as being out and amongst the people.

# Chapter 14: Get to Know Generation Z

No look towards the future of social media marketing would be complete without looking at who the characteristics of the primary future audience who the primary future audience will be. Generation Z is the up and coming generation that was born somewhere between 1998 and 2016 which means they range in age from 20 to 2 years of age. This means they are primed to take over the workforce in the coming years as they finish college and get to work on defining what the future will look like for them.

## *Foundational Events:*

The two major events of the 00s, the terrorist attacks on September 11 and the Great Recession have both had a significant impact on Generation Z, though unlike the Millennials that came before them they, at best, have a hazy memory of the event and its aftermath. Generally speaking, however, as a generation they have no concept of a time when the United States was not in a perpetual war with the poorly defined concept of global terrorism.

Meanwhile, the Great Recession cast a large shadow over the childhoods of many in Generation Z thanks to the financial stresses it likely put on their parents to varying degrees. Both events have likely left much of the generation with feelings of general unease and insecurity that will likely lead them to make more cautious, frugal choices, at least as they take their first steps out from the safety of their parent's shadows.

## *How They See Themselves:*

Generally speaking, Generation Z self-identifies as being determined, responsible, open-minded, thoughtful, compassionate and loyal. There is some dissonance between how they see themselves and how they see their peers, however, starting with the fact that they see their contemporaries as curious, adventuresome, spontaneous and competitive, all things they do not readily self-identify as.

Another interesting aspect of this generation is that their reading comprehension is off the charts thanks to their native familiarity with digital devices and content of all types. When it comes to religion, perhaps the most surprising thing about Generation Z is that it is shaping up to be the most religious generation in nearly a century with about 41 percent claiming some sort of religion compared to just 18 percent of Millennials, 21 percent of Generation X and 26 percent of Baby Boomers.

This may have something to do with why they appear to be more risk-averse to a number of activities traditionally associated with people their age. A 2013 study found that the oldest members of Generation Z were nearly 20 percent less likely to have tried alcohol than their peers in 1991. Safety concerns appear to be up as well as only about 8 percent never wore a seatbelt in 2013 as opposed to 26 percent of teens in 1991. Generation Z also has lower teen pregnancy rates and higher rates of high school graduation than their Millennial peers with Generation Z being 40 percent less likely to get pregnant in high school, 40 percent less likely to experiment with illegal drugs and 30 percent less likely to fail to graduate from high school at the planned time.

## How They Feel About Their Country:

One area where Generation Z is underperforming compared to those that have come before is when it comes to patriotism which likely has strong implications for how they are going to feel about the government for possibly all of their adult lives. They may well be interested in looking into alternatives that they feel do a more accurate job of reflecting their beliefs and feelings on inclusion.

It goes without saying that these findings will have strong implications for marketing of all types. While Generation Z looks to be far less likely to accept pro-American brands than generations past, they are going to naturally be more inclined to be interested in brands that actually do things differently. Research shows that there are three main factors that ultimately influence a generation: technology, societal norms, and age.

Overall, they tend to most closely resemble the millennials— which is hardly surprising—with the exception that they are far less optimistic about their future with nearly 70 percent expressing the opinion that the US is headed in the wrong direction and less than 30 percent claiming they felt the country was on the right track. When asked about how they felt overall, 44 percent said they felt worried, and 21 percent claimed they generally felt scared. Of those polled, only 12 percent came up with the adjective optimistic while at least a quarter of older generations felt this way. What's more interesting, perhaps, is that

71 percent felt their lives were about to get harder.

## *Always Online:*

The biggest shift for Generation Z is the fact that they have literally never known a world without the internet. In terms of content consumption, they are far more likely to stream their content in bite-sized chunks and are far more likely to watch content on their phone than on a television screen. In fact, they tend to avoid most television and movies and rarely consume any live programming that includes scheduled commercial break. As they have never watched traditional broadcast news or read a newspaper they are also far more likely than other generations to fall victim to hoaxes of all types.

When it comes to social media usage, just over 60 percent of millennials admit that social media plays a significant role in their lives, something that only 50 percent of Generation Z agrees with. One place where both generations agree, however, is when it comes to the level of public scrutiny available on social media. Roughly 60 percent of both generations admitted to being concerned with the fact that social media is too public which means their posts could eventually come back to haunt them. Of the two, Generation Z is letting this concern change their behavior with a noticeable trend towards more private social networks such as Snapchat.

Generation Z is also likely to share different types of information online than the generation before them and also to take more steps to protect their private information when appropriate. New trends are emerging that show they are also more likely to passively follow others on social media instead of sharing their own personal details. While they may not be completely happy with it, Generation Z continues to use Facebook as they see it as a vital way of connecting with their peers and friends. Generation Z is also one of the primary age groups that can be seen to actively be joining Twitter, largely because it is not something their parents are using in large numbers.

Snapchat has also gained a large amount of traction with this generation as it is much faster to send messages, pictures, and videos via Snaps, than through more traditional alternatives. Reliability and speed are two of the most important things to this generation which means that social media platforms that promise them are always going to gain popularity. While mobile technology and constant access to the internet are determining characteristics of this generation, they also seem perfectly adept at distinguishing between the online world and the world they inhabit when they are not online.

Generation Z tends to spend its time in some type of private communication with the people they interact with in the real world, while mostly using social media to keep up with what is going on in the world at large and maintaining secondary relationships. As a result of this usage pattern, Generation Z spends more time on their smartphones to the point that relationships first developing online has become standard, if not expected. They do not like the idea of using the anonymity provided by the internet to misrepresent themselves, however, and they don't like the idea of being asked to change to fit some predetermined idea of beauty.

## Other Issues:

Those members of Generation Z who are not yet in college

(which is most of them) most commonly have to deal with parents who don't approve of the ease with which their children have access to the unfettered wilderness of the internet. Meanwhile, Generation Z can be expected to chafe at the thought of being controlled in a space that they feel completely at home in as it is essentially their birthright. The experiences they have online and the friendships and other relationships they have there are as real to them as any other.

This online lifestyle is not without its potential drawbacks, however, and Generation Z is already proving to be generally less confident in face to face interactions simply because they have had fewer of them overall in their lifetime than previous generations. In a recent study, 72 percent of Generation Z respondents indicated that they are seriously concerned with the way in which each of their postings will be perceived by their personal social network despite still using social media every day. Meanwhile, 82 percent admitted to not posting something they originally planned to after considering the potential ramifications. Despite these numbers, only about 40 percent claimed to have regrets about an existing post.

While millennials generally do not claim that they view race as a contributing factor to their feelings about a given individual when asked if they currently had friends of a different race then them, only 69 percent of millennials answered in the affirmative. Meanwhile, 81 percent of Generation Z was able to answer this question in the affirmative. When it comes to dating outside their race, however, millennials still have Generation Z beat 45 percent to 35 percent. This disparity might be due to the fact that Generation Z is the most racially diverse generation in American history with 48 percent claiming some percentage of non-Caucasian heritage. This is up approximately 10 percent from the average for millennials.

This general policy of inclusion extends to those of different sexual orientations as well with approximately 8 percent more Generation Z'ers than millennials claiming to currently have friends of a different sexual orientation. This tracks with their ideas towards marriage as well, with a general preference for inclusion shown. Areas, where Generation Z seems to be towing the line, include environmental awareness, universal healthcare, and social security.

Another interesting area where Generation Z has more leeway than previous generations is when it comes to discipline. Less than 50 percent of Generation Z is or was regularly disciplined when they broke the rules at home and only about a quarter went to their parents for help on their homework.

# Conclusion

Thanks for making it through to the end of The Future of Social Media Marketing, let's hope it was informative and able to provide you with all of the tools you need to achieve your goals, whatever they may be. Just because you've finished this book doesn't mean there is nothing left to learn on the topic, and expanding your horizons is the only way to find the mastery you seek.

Now that you have reached the end of this book it is time to stop reading and start implementing your very own future-proof social media marketing plan. While you likely have ideas as to how to create or improve your presence across a wide variety of platforms, it is important to work on improving them one at a time instead of all at once. This way you will be able to devote your full resources to ensuring each platform is performance-ready before moving on to the next. After all, the goal is to create a social media marketing plan that will last for years to come; you certainly have the time to do things right.

Putting together the perfect social media marketing plan is no easy feat which means you need to commit to the process fully from the start with each new social media platform you take on. Finishing the job only halfway is not an option in this case as a partially completed social media profile, or one that is not updated frequently will only make your brand look dated and out of touch. This means that instead of trying to use every platform out there, you will find far more success by being selective and only getting started with the ones you know you are going to finish. Taking the long-term view on your social media marketing plan may mean getting started later, but the end results will be far more productive. After all, social media marketing is a marathon, not a sprint, which means that slow and steady wins the race each and every time.

Finally, if you found this book useful in any way, a review on Amazon is always appreciated!